RUNABOUT

Running Through my 50s

100 Marathons in 30 Countries

Cheryl Lynn Broas

RUNABOUT

Running Through my 50s

100 Marathons in 30 Countries

Cheryl Lynn Broas

First paperback edition 2021

Book design by Cheryl Lynn Broas

Photography by Robert Louis Cioppa

ISBN: 978-1-291-45489-5

I dedicate this book to:

My family, in particular my husband Bob, who encouraged my racing. He was the ultimate supporter; somehow delivering bags of ice during the heat of the Vermont City Marathon and warm coffee during the blizzard of the Ground Hog Day Marathon in Michigan. To my granddaughter, Josie, "May you find inspiration in the grittiness of your Grandma!"

Contents

Contents vii

Introduction.. 9

PART I: The Newbie.. 13

    Chapter 1: Edinburgh Marathon..................................... 15

    Chapter 2: Chicago Marathon... 19

    Chapter 3: Dublin Marathon... 25

    Chapter 4: Cornish Marathon... 31

    Chapter 5: Maui Oceanfront Marathon 37

    Chapter 6: Paris Marathon 43

    Chapter 7: Rotterdam Marathon 49

    Chapter 8: Antwerp 10 Miles & Marathon................... 53

    Chapter 9: Asics Stockholm Marathon 57

PART II: The Maniac-24 in 12 65

    Chapter 10: Tokyo Marathon 69

    Chapter 11: Virgin London Marathon 77

    Chapter 12: Riga Marathon 85

    Chapter 13: Copenhagen Marathon 91

    Chapter 14: ING Night Marathon Luxembourg 97

    Chapter 15: Laugavegur Ultra Marathon 103

    Chapter 16: Freedom's Run 113

    Chapter 17: Athens Authentic Marathon 117

    Chapter 18: Vodaphone Istanbul Marathon 121

Part III: The Speedster-Finding My Inner Rabbit 129

    Chapter 19: Bay of Fundy Marathon........................... 133

Chapter 20: Crater Lake Rim Run.................................139

Chapter 21: Tallinn Marathon 145

Chapter 22: Oslo Marathon 151

Chapter 23: Kigali International Peace Marathon.......157

Chapter 24: Race to The Tower 165

Chapter 25: Petrified Forest Marathon 171

Chapter 26: Firenze Marathon.................................177

PART IV: The Ultra Marathoner-More Than 26.2.................. 183

Chapter 27: Comrades Marathon.................................187

Chapter 28: Valencia Marathon.................................195

Chapter 29: Antelope Canyon Ultra Marathon 203

Chapter 30: Belfast Marathon.................................213

Chapter 31: Thunder Dragon Marathon 219

Chapter 32: Race to The Stones 229

Chapter 33: Arches Ultra-50K.................................235

Chapter 34: 2020 Publix Atlanta Marathon.................243

Chapter 35: Covid-19 Puts the Brakes On 251

Chapter 36: Round Reading Ultra Marathon 255

Chapter 37: 2020 Plym Trail Marathon.................259

Chapter 38: Not Quite London Marathon.................265

Afterword...273

Glossary of Terms 275

Acknowledgments 277

Introduction

In April 2008, my husband, Bob, and I retired from the field of architecture. Days later we left our home in New York for our dream trip, the circumnavigation of Vancouver Island in sea kayaks. Imagine traveling 2,000 miles across Canada on the VIA Rail train from Toronto to Vancouver with your folding sea kayaks, food, and gear. We took a ferry from Vancouver over to Vancouver Island, set up the kayaks, filled them with our "stuff" and the adventure began. We paddled 1,000 miles over four months sleeping on beaches, visiting remote light houses, Canadian parks, and Indian villages. We came back to New York in September feeling very strong and physically fit.

The next year we started a regular program of traveling to spend more time with our daughter in England. We focused our energy on gardening. Occasionally, we ventured out in our kayaks, but all the fitness and strength that we gained over the summer of 2008 became a distant memory. I had the best of intentions after retirement, I would get fit, get healthier, but there was no long-term strategy to get me there. I needed a spark to ignite the fire.

That spark came in the fall of 2010. Bob and I decided to go to a one-week retreat at a health spa with Bob's college roommate and his wife. The excuse for the trip was to kick-start a healthier lifestyle. After signing up, Bob and I quickly realized that we desperately needed the kick start; we were not fit enough to take part in the daily exercise program of dawn hikes, morning yoga & Pilates, and afternoon gym classes. We imagined ourselves sidelined after the first day!

We needed a quick, simple way to better our fitness before the retreat. Running seemed like the most efficient and cheapest way to get there. Bob and I purchased quality running shoes and thought we were ready to run. We barely made it a quarter-mile; my heart was leaping out of my chest. We regrouped and stepped out to run again the next day. We kept at it in preparation for the retreat. Many readers will wonder why I kept going!

     1. Fear was such a strong early motivator. When we realized we could not fully take part after giddily signing up for the life-altering retreat, we knew it was time to focus on our health. Ultimately, it was the feeling

of my heart throbbing after such a brief run that scared me into getting back out to run the next day, and the next.

2. Eventually, running became a social outlet. After retirement I started to feel isolated, missing the social aspects of my work community. I started signing up for local 5K races. I realized that there was a fellowship amongst runners and that camaraderie interested me. After seeing their shirts everywhere at the 2011 Stride 5K Run, I *"discovered"* NewRo Runners. They are now my home club and its members make up a significant part of my New York social network.

3. Runners inspire me. For example, my UK home club, The Looe Pioneers, is a run club of over 150 people in a small town of 5,000; 3% of the community participates! The club adopted me back in 2012 when they were just a handful of runners doing a few local races. In just a few years, the club has grown exponentially in size and breadth. The club's accomplishments are now published weekly in The Cornish Times! These inspiring members run every distance from local 5K road races to 100-mile trail races, they run, bike, swim, and in between they socialize and organize community projects.

4. I love the feeling of accomplishment as I cross the finish line of a race. I love checking the stats to see how I performed. Did I run better than in the last race? Did I place in my age group? In my youth, I was never involved in a sport long enough to become competitive but I have the bug and it has bloomed.

5. I had to find out what I was capable of. At first, it was the drive to complete one marathon. Did I have the endurance? What was my potential? I finished my first marathon and knew I could run another one faster. My niece, Carolyn, a race walker that qualified for the 2004 Olympic Track and Field Trials encouraged me to try for a Boston Marathon qualifying time, a "BQ." She encouraged me from the beginning of my marathon training to seek the elusive "sub-four." My BQ time for a woman age 50-54 was under four hours. Could I achieve my magic number!

Ten years later I am celebrating the completion of 100 races of marathon + distance. The question is, what kept me going? In retrospect, I found that I was heavily motivated by incremental goals and testing my limits. I rewarded myself with races. Luckily, I found some like-minded companions along the way:

1. The marathoning flood gates opened in 2013. I met Julia who was hoping to finish 52 marathons in one year. She introduced me to the idea of joining the Marathon Maniacs, a club of runners that do multiple marathons with minimal recovery time. I didn't think it was physically possible to run more than one or two marathons a year! I joined as Maniac #7682 in October of 2013. I spent a year running 24 marathons to become a Maniac with the second-highest club status of Platinum.

2. While surfing the internet, I stumbled upon the Marathon Globetrotters, a club of runners that enjoy traveling and running marathons in different countries. In 2014, I was accepted into the club after completing marathons in nine countries. By 2019 I had run marathons in 30 countries. I found a way to merge my love of travel with my love of running.

This book compiles my experiences running 38 of the 100 marathons. The maps below identify the states and countries where my 100 marathons were run. The blue represents countries or states where I ran a marathon but did not write a race report. The yellow represents countries or states where I ran a marathon and wrote a race report. The red dot shows the location of the race.

I ran 58 marathons in the USA:

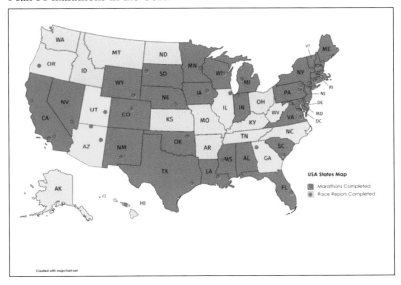

35 marathons in Europe:

and 7 marathons in other parts of the world:

      I didn't start writing race reports until I tried my first international marathon in Edinburgh, Scotland. Initially, I hoped that I could encourage my fellow runners to try foreign races in cities I came to love. Eventually, I hoped people would get excited about running in unusual places, National Parks, National Battlefields, Coastal Paths, and National Trails. I also thought that my running mates could learn from some of my mistakes... little did I know there would be plenty of mishaps along the way!

PART I: The Newbie

I went for a jog in the fall of 2010 and by 2011 I was racing local 5K's and loving the camaraderie. I tried my first half marathon in February 2012 at the Pecos Valley Stampede in Roswell, NM. I raced in the desert looking for opportunities for alien interaction in the UFO Capitol. I was hooked! Mysterious, Roswell is best known as the crash site of an alleged UFO in 1947 and alien references are everywhere. I loved seeing an unknown part of the country, spending time contemplating alien life while pursuing my new running hobby. I had not taken into account the impact of the 3,500' altitude. My race finish time of 2:22:56 was disappointing. I ran the NYC Half the next month in 2:02:47. I had a blast running through Times Square! As I compared the two races, I was learning lessons about the impact of running in unknown conditions like the New Mexican desert.

The 2012 Philadelphia Marathon was my first crack at the marathon distance. The race appealed to me because I spent five years traveling from my previous home in Virginia to work with a client in Philadelphia. Over the years, I developed a love for Philly. It's a city of strong contrasts, diverse neighborhoods like the Italian Southside, The Navy Yard, University City, and Rittenhouse Square. It is a city with a rich colonial history witnessed at the Liberty Bell and Independence Hall. I remember the great food halls at Reading Terminal, 30th Street Market, and of course the Italian market on 9th Street. I picked the race because the course landmarks had a personal meaning. We could expect the mayor to be standing at the finish line to congratulate runners as they crossed the finish. A big-city race with small-town touches seemed the perfect choice for my maiden run. The race starts and finishes by the Philadelphia Art Museum, so images of Rocky Balboa came to mind. I would play the song theme from Rocky when the going got rough!

2012 was the year of Hurricane Sandy; the New York City (NYC) Marathon was canceled at the last minute, so Philadelphia Marathon opened up spots for NYC Marathoners. As a result, my run club had more than a dozen entrants in Philly. With so many club mates there, I got to fully experience the social aspects of marathoning; taking part in club training runs, travel planning with my teammates, and best of all, sharing my enthusiasm during the race weekend pasta dinner and meet-ups.

I ran a strong race to mile 17, then hit the infamous "wall" and by mile 22, I was on the sideline with cramps. I was so angry! I felt robbed of my epic finish! I knew I could do much better! I had to try again, so I signed up for the LA Marathon. I built off my Philadelphia training so with 14 weeks to race day I spent the winter getting ready. Stronger and wiser, I finished fifteen minutes faster, but the sub-four finish still eluded me.

I ran my first NYC Marathon in November 2014. It was an incredible experience. My club had 34 runners in the race. I ran with a group of girlfriends and crossed the finish line side by side with my friend Mara! I was hooked and have run the course five times.

As a Newbie, I ran 17 marathons in 2 years and issued 9 race reports to document my experiences. The chart below sequentially lists my first seventeen marathons. The nine race reports are highlighted in grey:

	RACE	Date	Location	Time
1	Philadelphia Marathon	18-Nov-12	Philadelphia, PA	4:17:23
2	LA Marathon	17-Mar-13	Los Angeles, CA	4:02:24
3	Edinburgh Marathon	26-May-13	Edinburgh, UK	4:07:15
4	Chicago Marathon	13-Oct-13	Chicago, IL	3:59:02
5	Dublin Marathon	28-Oct-13	Dublin, IRL	4:16:57
6	Cornish Marathon	17-Nov-13	Pensilva, UK	4:30:39
7	Maui Oceanfront Marathon	19-Jan-14	Maui, HI	5:10:54
8	Central Park Marathon	23-Feb-14	New York, NY	4:09:46
9	Shamrock Marathon	16-Mar-14	Virginia Beach, VA	4:18:00
10	Paris Marathon	6-Apr-14	Paris, FRA	4:01:29
11	Rotterdam Marathon	13-Apr-14	Rotterdam, NLD	3:59:40
12	Antwerp Marathon	27-Apr-14	Antwerp, BEL	4:05:34
13	Stockholm Marathon	31-May-14	Stockholm, SWE	4:11:18
14	Helsinki City Marathon	16-Aug-14	Helsinki, FIN	4:15:45
15	Berlin Marathon	28-Sep-14	Berlin, DEU	4:08:04
16	Hartford Marathon	11-Oct-14	Hartford, CT	4:09:20
17	TCS NY City Marathon	2-Nov-14	New York, NY	4:10:50

Chapter 1: Edinburgh Marathon

Date: May 26, 2013, 10 am start, Edinburgh, Scotland

Weather: 55F and sunny

Participation: 8,197 marathoners, 19,000 in all the races

Run with the Ponies or Murder in Gosford Park...

I am running my third marathon and it's an international one. We are in Edinburgh, Scotland, the location of our honeymoon fifteen years ago. It's 8:30 am and we are leaving the hotel for the 1.5-mile walk to the race start. The weather is cool but comfortable. We got energized as soon as we stepped out of the hotel because we passed the relay exchange bus pick-up. There were frenetic runners all around us, so we quickened our pace! As we crossed the bridge over Waverly Train Station... we found the real crowds!

We had 40 minutes to the race start, so went straight to the toilets. I had

read that it was a flaw in the previous year. ~Not anymore! No lines for the men at all. They go to a separate area with screened open-air urinals. Women and selective men go to the porta-potty area with a single line. Volunteers man the line and hurry us to available toilets. I

15

went through the line twice and the longest wait was 10-minutes, excellent drill sergeant choreography from the volunteers!

This race claims to be the fastest course in the UK so I am here with high hopes for a fast run. The beginning of the race was fabulous, downhill, and great sightseeing. We start on Regent Road by Calton Hill, just below the US Consulate. We pass the Queen's official Scottish home, Holyrood Palace, across from the palace is the Scottish Parliament. We run through the extraordinary Holyrood Park with Arthurs Seat, the extinct volcano, and the Salisbury Crags. I've only run two miles! After five miles I arrived at the Firth of Forth waterfront with a speedy 8:15 pace!

We ran along the water to the town of Musselburgh at mile 8, the location of our finish. At mile 9 we move inland with occasional glimpses of the Firth of Forth, running by the oldest golf course in the world. Records show golf played here in 1672! Bob hoped to meet me at mile 13, but the bus from the start took much longer than expected. By the time he got off the bus and walked over, I was long gone and he was cheering for the masses and waiting for the elites to return to the finish.

After fourteen miles we were running aside trees with no sea views, so I chatted with the runners. We saw the elites on their return leg, the Kenyans and Ethiopians were in the lead! I kept cheering for them until we got to Gosford Park at mile 17.5. The stone gates of Gosford Park were beautiful, but then you look up to see speedsters popping out of the grounds... and... OMG... it's a dirt... track!! I love a trail run but not on the

course of the fastest marathon in the UK. This is my Boston qualifier!! I yelled out, "What the heck?!"

The first part of Gosford Park was nice, a small paved track, a path through the woods, but once we got past architect Robert Adams, Gosford House it was

downhill but ghastly conditions, large gravel for a half-mile, and for kicks, two supercharged horses galloping along the fence rails to make it look easy! I humorously called them "show-offs."

Mile 19 and we were headed back towards Musselburgh. I started to realize that a sub 4:00 was probably not going to happen. I was finding it very difficult to hold my pace. I was running past so many walkers, I hoped it wouldn't affect my drive to the finish.

It got exciting again as we got back into town, I was feeling stoked and predicting a 4:03 finish! I had less than two miles left! Then I FELL! I was flat on my face, stiff as a board; I couldn't get up. Two fellow runners raised me like a plank and checked that I was OK. I took a break while I thanked my rescuers, sorted my broken running watch, and stretched my cramping legs, and with a little movement, I was sort of OK.

I took off again, but the fall took the wind out of my sails. People were cheering me from mile 25 to the finish, but I could not find the magic to finish strong. I was sulking; I was so crushed. I crossed the finish in 4:07, a great time considering the fall, but not the BQ time I had worked for.

At the race finish, we get water, a medal, and a men's race shirt. Then we move out to the public area. The first tent was the beer tent, I laughed! There was a sea of charity tents and vendor tents, but no signs to get us to the family meeting area. I walked and walked in vain. I had asked for directions before I left the finish area, but the volunteer sent me in the opposite direction.

I sat on the ground to have a good pout when I saw the information tent. Those volunteers sent me in the right direction. Bob saw me and started

screaming my name. What joy!! I got my mojo back. We took this mocking, bloody hand, tough gal photo.

I hobbled back to the bus, a 25-minute walk, then rode 50 minutes to get back to the start, then walked 1.5-miles to the hotel. I was exhausted!! Take-out sushi and TV were all I could manage until I got a night's rest.

This could be a great race, but it wasn't my day... and that's OK. I learned I need to better understand the course I am planning to run. I focused on the early race and didn't understand the challenges of the late miles. A late-race fall is never a good thing, and that set me back. I need to deal with it better....it will happen again!

The next day, we did a little sightseeing in Edinburgh and then went east to stay at Greywalls Hotel, the site of our honeymoon. It is a Scottish Edwardian country house designed by the famous architect Sir Edwin Lutyens. Lutyens has always been a favorite of ours, and this may be one of his best works. The grounds at the adjacent Muirfield golf course were a buzz because they were preparing for the 142nd Open Championship. Edinburgh and Greywalls Hotel were every bit as special as we remembered!

Chapter 2: Chicago Marathon

Date: October 13, 2013, 9:15 am start, Chicago, Illinois

Weather: 46F

Participation: 40,230 marathoners

On The Ground Report.......

The Chicago Marathon is a super-fast flat course. I spent the summer training so I would peak for this race; It's been five months since my strong showing at the Edinburgh Marathon, my goal here is to finish under four hours and capture a Boston qualifying time! This is my first experience at a World Marathon Major, so the expectation is high. This race is "Gold" standard, so let's see if I can grab my gold...

I was methodical about my race apparel, wearing KT tape on both ankles, Saucony shoes, 1,000-mile blister-proof socks, shorts with the high thigh cut so no chaffing, Lululemon tank top plus my throwaway clothes, a t-shirt, tube sock arm warmers, and a beat-up old hat. I am looking very homeless but felt toasty warm, ready to tackle this course!

For nutrition, I packed up 3 Gu gels for miles 6, 12, and 18 plus two High5 gels for late in the race. I brought a bottle of water to carry for the first 8 miles. I plan to drink 8 oz per 30 minutes. I will drink 8 oz of Ultima a half hour before the race start. I will try a Gatorade electrolyte drink after miles 8 and 12 to see how my stomach handles it. The course will have Powerade gel at roughly mile 19 so I can stock up if need be.

Let the adventure begin.......

I left for the race on my own, my first time without Bob at the start line. He could not get into the park due to the security. The streets are quite empty, so I walk. I spot the Michigan Avenue bus and realize I should save my energy, so I hop on with a group of runners from Mexico knowing I had my emergency $20. The bus driver laughed at us for expecting change, wished us well, and gave us a free ride, love Chicago!!

I arrive at the security gates at 6:30 am but double back for a quick stop at Panera Bread...no toilet line for the ladies but the line for the mens is long ~jackpot! Next up security, no problem for me because I bring no bag to check. The bag check line was long. I hop in line for the toilets again, it moves fast and by 7:10 am the corrals open. I line up with the 3:55 pacers and have worn the pace group bib on my back. Getting into the corral, I quickly find my 3:55 group and set up my watch and iPod, then toss my extra shirt. My friend, Karen, magically finds me so we line up together before the corrals collapse. It's 7:30 and we are off!

Early on the course is not as crowded as I expected, but the bunching around the 3:55 pacers is crazy. All five pacers are running together and everyone is glued to them. I can't risk falling again, so get out ahead of them. I hope to join them again when things settle down.

Crossing the Chicago bridges is tough, my side of the bridge has no carpet, so we run on an open grate. It's hard on the feet and does slow me down. I love running through The Loop, loads of spectators, tall buildings, and the first miles go so fast! Soon we are through Old Town and see the historic Chicago Theater! I feel like it is such an easy run, I run with the 3:50 pacers, right behind them, and stay there.

Mile 4... WOW, there is Bob, on the sidelines, I scream and he sees me as I pass. The next time I look for him is mile 11. I settle in and just take in the sights. Soon enough we are up at Lincoln Park, I remember the zoo entrance from my childhood visit. I zoom through all the water stops, no need as I have my water bottle. People line the course with signs and

clever eye-catching paraphernalia. The best was an orange umbrella decorated with all kinds of orange junk, -who could miss it! There are photo faces, cowbells, and so much entertainment. I saw Elvis, a dozen military men throwing rifles in the air, cheerleaders, drag queens, and later in the race a Chinese drum band, a jazz band, ~it's showtime!

Mile 11... I am heading back downtown and I see Bob again. Incredibly, we find each other! I plan to see him again at mile 23. I just keep moving, staying a few minutes ahead of my 8:55 pace band splits.

I ditched the arm warmers and hat back at Mile 3. The need to pee has been with me from the start and it's not going away. I know better so I

keep drinking and refill my bottle at mile 8. I took my gel at mile 7 and tried Gatorade. I begin to look forward to mile 13 and the famous KPF building at 333 Wacker Drive, a favorite from my architecture school days.

Mile 13... I am feeling great, staying 2 minutes under my pace band and holding steady. Seems the training is paying off. Next up, the residential neighborhoods with a distinct character, Greektown, Little Italy, Pilsen, etc. The Tri-Berry Gu gel was not a good choice. Next time I will just buy chocolate, why look for variety when I always love chocolate and grumble about everything else. I still feel strong, but this is hard and I wonder why I signed up for the Dublin Marathon. What the heck was I thinking, get a BQ, and be done with it?

Why try to join the Marathon Maniacs? I am not a maniac, just a marathoner. How dumb was that? I better BQ because who wants to do this again??

Mile 16… I am still nailing my sub 9's but not gaining time anymore, I have lost the 3:50 pace group, and only rarely will one of their pacers sprint by me as he looks for the group. At this point, I see fellow marathoners with 3:45, 3:50, and even 4:20 pace group bibs. Everyone seems to be steady now, no one is passing, they just keep moving…

Mile 18… I have banked two minutes on my 3:55 pace band, now I can run a bit slower later on. Boy, I am looking good! If I slow to a 9:30 pace for the rest of the race, that's 8 miles, I achieve a finish of 3:57 by using my banked 2 minutes, perfect! I wonder how long my pace can last?

Gatorade is no longer an option; I dilute it with water, despite that, it's no good. That bite of banana is no good either. The 65-degree temperature is warmer than I like, I stay in the shade as much as possible. I slow along the boulevard in Pilsen for the cameraman, smile wave and he missed my picture. ~oh well, next one! My chocolate Gu went down well. No blisters, 1,000-mile socks might live up to the hype. No chafing, all Ok!!

Mile 20… I am no longer posting sub 9's. It's starting to get hard! I feel I can slow down; six more miles left and I am still ahead of the 3:55 pace group. I wonder where they are? Three more miles to Bob. I decide to pitch the water bottle, my arm is tired and I can use the water stops. The scenery is not so great now, the freeway on one side, warehouses on the other. We should be arriving in Chinatown soon!

Mile 21… I like the water stops, a nice distraction, a mental and physical break. They are two blocks long, the first block for Gatorade, the next block for water. It seems like we go by them quite often.

Mile 22… I should look for Bob now. I try to stay in the shade and check out the scenery. It's a bit gritty. I should have taken in more scenery earlier in the race. The 3:55 pace group passes me. I tried staying with them for a while, but it was just too much speed this late in the course. My 3:55 pace band says mile 22 @ 3:17, I am at 3:17:38, slowing down but still ok for a sub-four.

Mile 23… Where's Waldo… oops… Where's Bob? It is so confusing. There are so many turns here and I just don't see him yet there are not many people. I'm definitely in a runner's fog! I am so tired, so I walked a bit at the water stop.

Mile 24.9... I check the pace band, holy cow, I am now 3 minutes behind my 3:55 pace band.... what did I do? I wasted so much time, will I make a BQ time? How can this be, 2 minutes to spare for a 4:00 marathon... ugh... I can't hold a 9:00 pace and who knows where I am with the Garmin distance readings.... panic sets in!!

Mile 25... I can't even hold 9:30, I must move even faster, these miles are taking so long. Ugh, I am cursed!

Mile 26... A hill!? ~which is just the overpass to get into Grant Park but my heart is leaping from my chest,

800 meters to go and my watch says 3:57:00?? I can do 800 in 01:50 but not now! ~no way~ MOVE IT, GIRL, move it, move it!! I cross the finish with 3:59:02. So close and so much harder than expected. I trained so hard and yet the difference between LA and Chicago is just 3 minutes!

Post-race I have so many performance questions and no answers. I had low iron levels again two weeks before this race so that is a factor. My chest is congested from allergies so that is a factor, but with a flat course, I expected to do 3:55/3:57. My brain's desire to stop running at mile 23 was so strong, I responded to any excuse to slow down. I thought I had time to burn, I stopped for water and walked a bit, what a mistake! On the upside, the fear of failure at miles 25 and beyond pulled me back into race mode, what an adventure!

We spent time enjoying Chicago. Post-race we had drinks at the top of the John Hancock building. It was close to the hotel and made for the perfect celebration. We looked down into the warren of buildings and had a toast, "We run this city!" The next day, Bob and I joined Tracie and Karen for a Chicago River boat tour, another very worthwhile way to see Chicago.

It's a great town for high-rise architecture, we did walking tours to see the best of it. I was finally able to see Frank Lloyd Wright's projects in Oak Park on a tour with the Chicago Architectural Center. It had been on my "must-do" list since college! What a fabulous race experience and an architect's dream destination!

Postscript: I did get the illusive sub-four in Chicago and realized it was a huge accomplishment. It took time to sink in.

I was so excited to apply for the 2015 Boston Marathon, entering as soon as applications were open. Acceptance to run the Boston Marathon works on a rolling admission system, the fastest qualified runners per age group (for me that was a sub-four marathon) gain admission until all spots are filled. The cut-off time for those accepted changes every year so you are never guaranteed an entry.

I received notification from the Boston Marathon that I missed the cut-off by four seconds! I was shattered, ~four seconds!!! Why did I let myself walk at those water stations? I shed a tear feeling quite sorry for myself. I did not give up.

It took another year, but in December 2014, I finally got the outcome I was looking for, 3:56:42 at the California International Marathon. I applied for the 2016 Boston Marathon. The cut-off in Boston for 2016 was 3:57:32. Boston Athletic Association finally accepted me!

In September 2012, my niece planted the goal of running the Boston Marathon in my head. She is a world-class race walker with an eye for sports performance. She saw a potential that I had not taken notice of. It did not happen overnight, but working two years to hit that goal made it ever so meaningful. 550,000 people finish a marathon each year, 23,000 get to run the Boston Marathon by qualifying, now I am part of that 4%!

Chapter 3: Dublin Marathon

Date: October 28, 2013, 9:15 am start, Dublin, Ireland

Weather: 46F, 25 mph WSW wind, 83% humidity

Participation: 12,284 marathoners

Ready, Set, Don't Go, Go...

In the days leading up to the Dublin Marathon, we tracked the St. Jude Super Storm as it barreled towards Ireland. It took a last-minute turn, causing damage to the UK with 100 mph winds and several deaths. Dublin received 25 mph winds, sunshine, and cool temperatures. We picked a great weekend to leave the UK and visit Ireland!

I am a beekeeper. The day before our trip to Dublin, a member of my hive found a little hole in my net hood while I was doing a hive check. My bee friend taught me a painful lesson; it stung me just below the eye. It took about two hours for my face to transform. Swollen, disfigured, and unrecognizable, I wondered... would passport control let me into Ireland?

The next morning, I woke up less disfigured, hmm, OK, ready, set, let's go!

We flew into Dublin for some pre-race sightseeing, Trinity College and the Book of Kells were at the top of my list. I would run my race and then we would pick up a rental car to work our way south with visits to Kilkenny for the famous castle, Kinsale a foodie town just below Waterford with a historic port, the gorgeous Ring of Kerry, and the remote Dingle Peninsula. On the drive back we would go through the mountains to the Tarbert Ferry over to County Clare to see the Cliffs of Mohar and the moonlike limestone landscape of the Burren.

Let the adventure begin...

My fellow NewRo Runner, Mark, is running the marathon too. We met up for a pre-race dinner, swapping Dublin experiences, and sharing race plans.

As the race guide suggested I arrived at the start an hour early, but it was clear that we arrived way too early. It was windy, very windy, cold and there was no one around! An hour later, I was shivering. My legs feel like lead and I don't want to move! I strip down reluctantly, move into the pack, and pray for a quick start. It's 9:15 and we are off......

The pack quickly spreads out. The streets are dense with cheering supporters. I enjoy passing so many of the sights we saw over the last few days. We run by St. Stephan's Green and then by the Museum of Archaeology where we saw the "2,000-year-old bog men." One man, found in a bog in central Ireland, was so well preserved that his discovery caused a police murder investigation until archaeologists were called and dated his body to the Iron Age. I am warming up and my muscles are firing as I run by Trinity College, home of the Book of Kells. I marvel at the buildings, study the runners around me and think about the illuminated images in the "Book".

We cross the River Liffey to head up O'Connell Street. This area of Dublin is Georgian and has a different feel. We run on a wide avenue with cheering spectators lining the course. I know that Mark's wife Cathy will be here at the Parnell Monument to cheer so I look for her but no luck. I see the Gate Theater, then the Garden of Remembrance and the Writers Museum, all familiar from yesterday's sightseeing. It is only mile two but I feel better than expected given it's only been two weeks since the Chicago Marathon. I try to hold myself at the four-hour pace groups 9:09 pace. Does it feel like a good time to test out the theory of slow start stronger finish?? We pass the Hugh Lane Gallery; I think about the delight in Bob's eyes when we saw the studio of his favorite artist, Francis Bacon, recreated in the gallery.

We head further north, further than we ventured on foot. It looks and feels very similar to the neighborhood we drove with Bob's friend, Maria, a few days ago. Low-scale rowhouses line the street. It's a little gritty but there is a nice feel to the area. We are headed over to Phoenix Park for miles 4 - 8. If I still feel good leaving the park there may be some promise in this marathon!

We head into the park and run its paths which tightens up the pack. The park is lovely, a welcome contrast to the urban streetscape. As we reach the park's 1.5-mile long Chesterfield Avenue, the full effect of the gusting wind hits us... Wow! There are distractions, the trees lining the avenue are stately with massive trunks. Each tree becomes a potty for the unencumbered, even women are finding relief! We pass the Wellington Monument and the US Ambassadors' home. Is he out cheering for us??

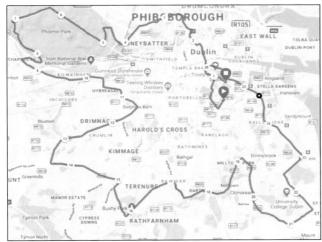 We leave the park and some of the gusting wind behind us. I am back in familiar territory as we go by mile 10 and I see the famous Kilmainham Gaol (jail). I met Marathon Maniac, Marsha White, and her husband Darcey there. She has run over 100 marathons approaching each one as a very fast walk. She plans to do this race in 6 hours. We toured the old jail together, fast friends. If I can finish this race, I too will join the Marathon Maniac club, I am so motivated and excited.... tally ho!!

As I move back out towards the South Circular Road, I am slightly ahead of the four-hour pace group; I feel OK but not as strong as I did in Chicago. At mile 11, we cross the canal. The scenery is lacking and so are the crowds. I ran along the canal two days ago and wonder how close I got to this intersection. I love Garmin Connect! When I get home, I will look up the race route and check for the overlap with my earlier runs here.

At mile 12, the four-hour pace group overwhelms me. I pull to the side, let them pass, and use the porta-potty. It feels good to stop, and that's scary? I re-commit to the run but also realize I want to enjoy this race. I will not suffer. I will keep it fun!

We still see cheering spectators. It is not as exuberant as the LA or Chicago marathons, but I make eye contact with people, give a high five, and thank them as I run. At mile 13.1 I post 2:01:05, I am pleased that I can do this well with two weeks of recovery from my fast Chicago run.

Bob will be at mile 18. If I can make it to him, then I know I will finish, I will join the Maniacs. There are very few costumes in this race, but lots of charity runners, each with a story to share, and fortunately the Irish seem to be skilled storytellers. The sun is out, temperatures warmed up; the weather is perfect except for the wind. I think about Mark, he should be past Bob by now. I hope he is enjoying this as much as I am!

We are running through lovely tree-lined boulevards, past Irish neighborhood pubs and shops. The field has thinned out and there is plenty of room to move about. I am starting to feel challenged. I will hold my pace, running hard until I see Bob. I will tell him to expect a 4:10 to 4:20 finish. It's better than the 4:45 pace I had envisioned.

I accelerate downhill to mile 18. I find Bob. I feel joy and relief, but also angst because the infamous Clonskeagh Hill is next. It's Dublin's version of Boston's Heartbreak Hill. We hug, I let him know I am backing off and he cheers me for my efforts. I slow it down and take the hill with a much slower stride.

The 4:10 pacers pass me after mile 21. It's to be expected, but still a letdown. I kick it in, step it up a notch. I bring it back up to a 9:45 pace but mile 23 presents challenges; I stop again for a bathroom break. I remind myself that this race is for fun as I post an 11:45 mile. I enjoy a mile of embassies... Japan, The Netherlands, India, China, UK, and finally the iconic but controversial US Embassy. Imagine a rotunda, with a moat and a twisted precast concrete open structure, a "sinewy drum." In the 1960s they loved it in Ireland but the modern design got mixed reviews in the USA, it was ahead of its time! The security fences and removal of the moat have not increased the building's charm!

We are getting close to our hotel and the finish. I pick up the pace again while others around me are walking. Fortunately, the wind is now just a light breeze! I see the Alliance Building, an old gasometer building converted to apartments. I saw it on one of my morning runs, and that familiarity gives me a surge of energy.

I run by our hotel. There are a few more spectators. Once I am over the canal bridge, our last "hill", the course moves by quickly. It's mile 25, the crowd's increase but in a half-mile, as we approach Trinity College the crowds swell to several deep and I hear a roar. I am starting to get passed by runners who have found a second wind. I hear loud music. We run around the perimeter of Trinity College. Cheering, crazy signs, this is so much fun! I see the finish and try to speed up but there is not much in my tank. It seems to take so long to cross the line but there it is 4:16:55!!

I need to keep walking to stop any cramping but I feel so much better than the finish at Chicago. Is it the slower pace? Is my body getting used to the distance? This race was fun except for the long cold wait at the start. We move through to get our medals. The volunteers are smiling and offer many congratulations. They boost our pride. We pick up the long sleeve race shirt... very nice, but sadly no women's cut. We get the goody bag, strangely filled with Oreos, Jelly Beans, and nothing healthy?? We are moved around Merrion Square until we exit to the family meet-up area. There are no official pictures or heat blankets.

It takes a long time for Bob to find me but I wait and watch the other

runners. They seem to move out quickly. There is no beer tent, just a few scattered tents with coffee and drinks for sale. This is not the after-party we had in Chicago or Philly. ~everyone heads for home!

We walk back towards the hotel and sit at our new favorite coffee shop 3fE at mile 25. We warm-up drinking coffee, then have a meal and watch for Marsha White. We should see her but never do.

I did it…. I ran two marathons in fifteen days! I qualified for entry into the Marathon Maniacs club at the first level, bronze. I can move up to the silver level of the club by running more marathons, six in six months. I can do that! I am so excited to order my kit, a pink diva-style tank top!

I learn that Bob saw Mark sprinting by at mile 18 with a look of intensity and determination. He finished with 3:26, 7:52 pace. As a male 50-55, he has a four-minute safety net below his Boston qualifying time! When I see him later, we hear his story? He ran hard but was not feeling well. At mile 25.75 his stomach lost its contents. He ran through it but I doubt that the spectators will forget his courageous drive to the finish. I may need to push a little harder next time!

I learn the next day that the winners were both Irish, the first time in over 20 years. The African elites passed the race up this year because it had trouble getting sponsorship. We also learned that a 27-year old first-time runner died after crossing the finish line. They had a death at the Dublin Half too so this is a very difficult year for Dublin's running community.

Would I recommend this race? I enjoyed it. The entire course was scenic and a great way to see Dublin. The spectators were vocal and well distributed along the course. The field was not crowded but I always had company along the route. I think the weather could be tricky but that is October racing and it adds to the ambiance! ~Touring around Ireland was spectacular and a great reason to run this race...

Chapter 4: Cornish Marathon

Date: November 17, 2013, 10:00 am start, Pensilva, UK

Weather: 46F start, 48F finish, light wind, overcast

Participation: 294 marathoners

Here it is Hills and History….

I wake up in my bed at home an hour before the alarm. I am nervous about this race...3 marathons in 35 days, the first one for time, the second to become a Marathon Maniac, and this one to push my boundaries. This racecourse will be tough and I am concerned, ~can I do it? Bob has me pledged to run the entire race, no walking. Luckily, the weather is in my favor, cool and overcast; this race is notorious for stormy wet weather.

I have time for a warm shower to loosen up the muscles, then it's my routine of beet juice, oatmeal, and banana. I ate lots of extra calories the last few days, I read that adding an extra 600 calories per day for the two days leading up to the race should help me avoid bonking or "hitting the wall". I want to see if the notorious miles 22-26 will be easier??

The race has a 10:00 am start so we arrive at 9:30 to pick up my bib and goody bag. What a different feel this race has, 299 people registered to run versus 40,000 in Chicago, 13,000 in Dublin.

 The start is in the village of Pensilva, our gateway to the Bodmin Moors in the Southwest England's County Cornwall, an area of highlands with acidic soil, rocky outcrops, low growing grasses, and lots of rain. The organizers have us inside the Millennium House, a local community center with toilets, showers, and meeting rooms. We all stay warm. What a perk!!

I line up at the back of the pack. This will not be a speedy race for me! I know these Cornish runners and they are a hardy lot. They run these hills daily and are much stronger hill climbers than me. I will increase my finish time starting in the back, but for me this one is about proving my endurance, getting over the hills, and staying mentally strong.

This marathon is "without a doubt one of the toughest in the UK, with over 2,400 feet of climbing, and much of this occurring after the critical 20-mile point" according to the *Cornish Guardian* newspaper. It will be the toughest race I have attempted. As I line up for the start Bob reminds me of a race safety rule, absolutely no headphones allowed! Panic sets in as he takes my iPod. I have never run a race without music. What will I do by mile 14? How will I pass the miles? He reminds me, "safety first!"

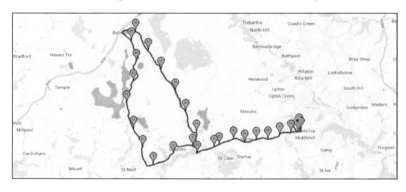

It is 10:00 am and we head out for two, one-mile laps around Pensilva. I like this because it gives me a chance to see Bob and I am already handing him my gloves. After two laps I am at a sub 9:00 pace, buzzing, and feeling too good.

We head out of town and hit our first hill. We climb 150' over the mile and reach a scenic viewpoint at mile 3. I take it in, you can see for miles! Then I remember we climb this hill to head

back to the finish, ouch! Off to the left are the iconic crumbling smokestacks from the long-gone era of Cornish tin mining. Smokestacks dot the landscape in the moors, even more so a few miles north in the village of Minions.

I settle in for the descent over the next mile and a half into the villages of Crow's Nest and Darite. The pack seems to have stretched out. At Darite, the Brownies are manning the water stops! They quickly hand us cups of water and offer gummy bears. I take a bear, give thanks and store him in my pocket for a boost later on! We hit the next hill coming out of Darite, a 200' climb. I am still running strong and clocking 9:30 even on the climb. I do not pass anyone; these Cornish runners are sailing over the hills with no complaints.

After mile 5, we are on a long downhill for the next three miles. I meet some interesting runners, a man with a 100 Marathons UK shirt, he falls in with another runner just ahead of me and talks about his love of marathons; it is his time to be social and meet people. I talk with a few more runners that have done this race; they warn me to save something for the last few miles. I will try but I am in new territory with my 3 marathons in 35 days. They wish me luck and we move on. No headphones = more chatting! The field is primarily Cornish club runners, Plymouth Musketeers, Tamar Trotters, Hayle Runners, Bodmin Women's Running Club…. no other New York runners. I must work on that!

At mile 6, we run over the Fowey River bridge to cheers from a group of supporters. This is the start point for the hike to Golitha Falls. Bob and I must come back. I love a good waterfall!

Suddenly there are lots of cars on this one-track lane, is it Sunday traffic? The end of church service? I realize the traffic is for us... the Pensilva spectators returned to their cars, and now they head out to cheer. Like Bob, they are driving to mile 16, the location of the famous Jamaica Inn. The line of cars continues. The windows are rolled down; I hear the music, the kids cheering and the horns sounding off. I have come to a spot where the lane is so narrow that we can't all proceed. An oncoming car cannot pass by so all the cars must reverse. They are looking for a wide spot in the road so they can let the oncoming traffic pass. I run by enjoying the show!

At mile 8 we are almost at the elevation low point of the race. Next is a two-mile 400' climb to the race high point and then relatively smooth sailing for miles and miles... yippee! I believe I can do this; I feel really good. I do not miss the headphones. I listen to conversations, listen for cars, listen to the cheering from the sidelines.

By mile 11 we start to see the lakes out on the moors, the views are spectacular, long open vistas, patches of farmland amongst open rolling hills. Just a little chill to the wind so I'm glad to have arm warmers that I can pull up and down as needed.

Mile 13.1... Cockle doodle do... mid-way and I am trumpeted by a cockerel. I marvel at how memorable that is. I clock in at 2:07, a good time with my weakness on the hills. It will not be my fastest marathon but who knows... maybe a 4:20? How great would that be!

Mile 13.5 and we see Dozmary Pool. It is associated with the legends of King Arthur and the Knights of the Round Table. This area is thought to be the home of the Lady of the Lake. One legend claims that King Arthur rowed out to the Lady of the  Lake and received the sword Excalibur from her rather than pulling the sword from a stone. Sir Bedivere threw Excalibur back into Dozmary Pool after King Arthur was mortally wounded. We are on the moors running amongst legend.

Mile 14, I see Roger Carter, he leads my local running club, the Looe Pioneers. Like many others, he is riding a bike. The race staffs the route with bikers, they talk to us, cheers us, and keep an eye on us. Such a great idea in an isolated setting!

I look forward to seeing Bob. He is waiting for me at the famous Jamaica Inn, mile 15.5. Why famous you ask? In 1936 the English author, Daphne du Maurier, published a novel titled "Jamaica Inn." A gritty period piece that was made into a film by Alfred Hitchcock in 1939 starring Maureen O'Hara. The Inn is now a famous watering hole and a great spot to stop for lunch while touring around the moors. In the photo, I am cruising in to pick up my snacks and some words of encouragement.

Mile 16 to 22 is a complete change of scenery. We run gently downhill along the Fowey River valley. I run a good portion of this leg with very little company, but a few people are still cheering us on. I feel great and find it so picturesque. I admit to missing my headphones, my leg turnover would be faster if I was listening to the Rocky Theme song, Gonna Fly Now, on this downhill!

At mile 19 I see something that is a first for me, a sign for otters crossing! Here is an example of the sign. I kept a lookout for the next few miles, but no sightings for me!

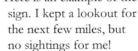

At mile 21, I am expecting to hit "the wall" but I feel good. The hills are coming. Can I fulfill my promise to Bob with no walking??

NOT LONG NOW was painted on the road just as we tackle the 200' climb at mile 22, sweet!

At mile 22.5, I see King Doniert's Stone, small pieces of two beautifully carved 9th-century Celtic crosses that celebrate the Celtic King Dumgarth, who ruled the kingdom of Cornwall, Devon & Somerset until he died in 875 AD. It's been 1150 years; the stones still stand homage on the moors!

I peak over the last 200' climb at mile 25.5 fully knowing I did it, never walking, never hit the wall. I am not sure I could tackle another hill, but I don't have to...it's downhill from here. I am spent, but I feel so good. I see Bob as I head to the finish, and he captures the moment. I finish with a time of 4:29:12, my slowest time by 12 minutes, but I consider it a huge win, one of my best efforts. This is my home county race and I will be back again!

Chapter 5: Maui Oceanfront Marathon

Date: January 19, 2014, 5 am start, Maui, Hawaii, USA

Weather: Sunny with 63F at the start, 79F at the finish

Participation: 440/marathoners, 529/half marathoners, 188/10K, and 172/5K

Running to get Maui'd......

Our friends, Julia and Shane, selected the Maui Oceanfront Marathon as their destination wedding venue. With palm trees, sandy beaches, and blue ocean waves lapping the shoreline, what could be more romantic? Add in humpback whales, the sound of the conk shell, Haku (head) lei's, lots of sunshine and the atmosphere grows! Run 17 miles to prepare your mind for the marriage ceremony and one will experience something truly unique. The anticipation grows tenfold when you are asked to be a running bridesmaid! Consider our east coast winter and this race is a gift from the Hawaiian gods!

As a bridesmaid, my job was to ease the stress of being a bride. Pitch in! It was time to put my skills to work. Julia had a plan for acquiring her perfect running bridal gown, so I went to work on the headdress. I was fortunate enough to recruit our milliner daughter to make the veil. The bridesmaid's headpiece would be my handiwork. Julia was looking for things old, new, borrowed, and blue, so the veil was made from an antique one. After running 17 miles, Julia and her veil were still picture perfect!

The race starts at The Shops at Wailea at 5 am, an early start to beat the heat of the day. It's a point-to-point course running along the shoreline to Old Lahaina Town. The streets are open to traffic so runners stay on the shoulder of the road. The few cars we saw were out cheering for us!

This was the first time I ran with makeup! The maid of honor is dressed in a yellow Marathon Maniac shirt, one bridesmaid wore blue and two bridesmaids wore the pink diva Marathon Maniac shirt. The wedding party ran together for most of the 17 miles to Papalaua Beach Park, the site of the wedding ceremony.

The first seven miles take us through the towns of Wailea and Kihei. It is dark so the street lighting is greatly appreciated. The wedding party drew lots of cheers and the spectators kept asking about the upcoming nuptials. So much chatting, laughing, and interacting with the spectators and other runners made the first-hour zoom by!

At 6:15 we leave the townscape and start to see the National Wildlife Refuge north of town. It is our first taste of the more native and undeveloped land of Maui. Our senses are heightened as we see the white sand beach, hear the sound of waves and smell the mix of salty air and the boggy ponds. Directly ahead we can see the wall of the West Maui Mountains. Sunrise is at 7:00 am so slowly we start to comprehend the beauty around us.

I notice that the mile markers are counting down to the finish, 14, 13, 12, etc., a first for me in a race. By Mile 12 we are on the Honoapiilani Highway and we see The Maui Ocean Center; the real prize is a festive aid station offering water and ice lolly sticks. We runners will be voting for the best aid station after the race and so far, this one has my vote!

The sun is up and the temperatures are starting to rise. The wedding party has spread out, it's much quieter now as everyone is starting to think about the upcoming nuptials. We have just 45 minutes before we need to be on the beach ready to witness the traditional Hawaiian wedding ceremony for Julia and Shane. Bob and the other non-runner guests will already be there to help set up and cheer on our arrival.

McGregor Point Lighthouse Scenic Viewpoint at mile 13 is one of the best places to see humpback whales. We are here during the winter migration, so the whale watch begins. At mile 14, we hit the jackpot! I hear the powerful exhaling of a whale quite close to the shore, right off

the rocky point in this photograph. The bridal party gets an aquatic escort to the wedding at Papalaua Beach!!

We arrive and the park is full of pre-wedding activities. The Kahuna Pule (traditional Hawaiian wedding officiant) is ready for us. The bridesmaids quickly don white togas for the ceremony.

We share a few emotional moments before Miss becomes Mrs.

We take a quick post-wedding photo before getting back on the course, a mere 32-minute delay but a life-changing experience!

I ran the last miles with my fellow bridesmaid, Karen, leaving the bride and groom to run with the other well-wishers. During miles 17-22 we basked in the ceremony's afterglow, but the Hawaiian heat drained me. We passed through my new favorite aid station, "Break Through the Wall." Karen and the aid station volunteers revived me with a cup of ice. Surely, I would not have kept running without it. The last four miles had little tree cover, and I was still overheating. Somehow, we missed the turn off the highway at mile 25.5 and carried on until Karen flagged down a passing car to direct us back to the race finish. ~Halleluiah, we made it!

I met up with the rest of our contingent from NewRo Runners, enjoyed a little time at the free massage tables, and then found the wedding party celebrating at Spanky's Riptide, Maui's 5-star dive bar. Then it's the Old Lahaina Hawaiian Luau for a traditional feast/wedding dinner and hula dancing show.

~What a memory!

We combined the marathon with adventures in Maui: Driving up to the 10,000-foot dormant volcano at Haleakala National Park for a view of the sunrise and a hike into the largest crater in the world. Diving the Molokini Crater off the coast of Wailea, hearing the songs of the humpback whales as green sea turtles swam by! It took rocking winter waves to force us, divers, back to shore. We flew in a helicopter over west Maui on an unforgettable ride to the island of Molokai to see the tallest sea cliffs in the world. On a mission to find the best banana bread in Maui, the west coast rewarded us with blowholes and the breadwinner. As suggested in every guide book, we drove the 50-mile corkscrew Hana Highway for lush

vistas, waterfalls, fresh coconut, and an overnight stay at the sumptuous Hana Hotel.

We flew to the big island of Hawaii to dive with manta rays! The sea gods brought tall waves, so they canceled our dive. ~onwards to

Kilauea Visitor
Center for the active
volcano. We saw the
glowing red crater at
night!

We capped the
Hawai'i Volcanoes
National Park trip with a
recovery run at Kīlauea
caldera. l started at the
Kilauea Overlook and
hugged the crater's edge
following the Kau Desert
Trail through the steam
and sulfur vents on the
Steaming Bluff. I passed
the Kilauea Visitor Center
and then dropped down
into the rain forest on the
Halema'uma'u Trail, over
the Kīlauea Iki Trail black
lava field to end in the
Thurston Lava Tube! ~5.5
miles of crazy cool.

The best run ever!

Chapter 6: Paris Marathon

Date: April 6, 2014, 8:35 am start, Paris, France

Weather: 55F and sunny

Participation: 39,135 marathoners

Ahh, Gay Paree... I wonder.... will I be gay at the race finish???

Our daughter and her husband have joined us on this trip to Paris. Jess is six months pregnant, so this is a big family travel celebration. We are staying less than a mile from the race start in a small boutique hotel just north of the Trocadero. It's perfect for me to access the start while Bob, Jim, and Jessica have easy access to cheer at mile 18. Jim was planning to join me for miles 18-23 to help get me through my problem miles but a bout of food poisoning has put that into question??

I am recovering from bronchitis I picked up after the Shamrock Marathon in Virginia three weeks ago. It forced me to take off from my training for

two weeks. I planned to beat my Chicago time of 3:59:02 but that seems unlikely. My excitement level is high, I feel good, and it is so inspiring to have the family here cheering me on! Let's see what unfolds today...

Bob and I head out to the start. They set the corrals up on the Champs-Élysées, just below the Arch du Triomphe. My 4-hour corral is right in front of Louis Vuitton! The only toilets I see are in the corral, two for hundreds of runners.

What a line! One can only imagine what inappropriate behavior that leads to, so I hope it rains this evening! I settle in and wait 45 minutes for my corral to start, finally heading out at 9:20 am.

The first few miles are a slow downhill over brick pavers with wall-to-wall cheering spectators. We run by the Grande Palais, the Petit Palais, and through the Place de la Concorde with its tall obelisk. It is spectacular with the trees in flower!

At 3k, we are running by the Louvre. Seeing the building rouses my spirit. Next up, the Rue di Rivoli, I remember this area from my college days. I laugh as I run by the Hotel de Ville. Old buildings never change. It looks exactly as I remember it from 25 years ago!

At 5k, we run around the Bastille, a big traffic circle. I can't believe that they have shut this circle to make way for us runners. Traffic must damn us. I settle into an 8:50 pace and enjoy the center city. Cheering spectators and six-story buildings line the street. We hit the first water stop, which offers bottled Vittel water and bottle recycling. ~very nice! I carry my water bottle to avoid stopping but am impressed by the orderliness!

At 10k we enter Bois de Vincennes, the park we will traverse for the next 7 k. We see Chateau de Vincennes, the medieval royal palace before Louis XIV made the move to Versailles. We are entertained by lots of different bands. We can hear heavy drums pulsating all through the park. I am feeling quite good so continue to hold my pace. I start fueling with both gel and dates. I am hoping dates will stave off the feeling of hunger later on. The water stops offer oranges, bananas, raisins, and sugar cubes. The fruit is popular so the course is filled with banana and orange peels! Keep your focus on the marathon obstacle course! Still, no toilets and people make do at every tree along the way.

We exit the park, back to the city streets. We have spectators again, many of them cheering... ALLEZ, ALLEZ, ALLEZ... love that sound! At 23k we pop out along the Seine and take in a gorgeous view of the apse of Notre Dame and then the Palais de Justice. People are sitting on the bridges cheering us on; it's energizing! The sun is shining and the heat is getting to be a bit much. I have started using the water stops to dump water on my head. The clouds are rolling in, just what I need!

At 26k we go into the famous Lady Diana tunnel, it runs for a half-mile and I am not liking this. It's so dark I cannot see where I am stepping! Further on there is a flashing light show. It's very disorienting but thankfully it does not last long!! We depart the tunnel and the reward is a glimpse of the Eiffel Tower, sweet!

I am starting to feel some GI issues, my colon is burning, it's way too early for this? I still run strong and I start thinking of Bob, Jim, and Jess. I will see them after the Trocadero. I am so excited; I hope I can pick them out of the crowd.

The Trocadero is bursting with activity! I pass the medical station. It's the first time I have seen an assembly line of seated runners getting calf massages from the medical staff. Runners are stopping to fuel up but I just want to tear through here to see my family in a half-mile. My GI is still burning. Maybe I should lay off the speed, or maybe just go for it? I have done 18 miles at a great pace... if I can keep this up, I can coast the next two marathons in April??? Gosh, am I bargaining with myself now??

I get to 29.5k, mile 18.5, and see Bob smiling and waving. What??? Jim is ready to run! I can't believe it... a decision is made... I will go for it! I get to the team and wave off the extra gels, headphones, even forget to leave my hat. Jim and I carry on together. I feel so energized! The course gets crowded at this point; the streets are not as wide and I get stuck behind runners. Jim weaves through but I am saving my energy. I am gauging the severity of the GI and wondering if we are going uphill? I am slowing down but still cruising past my fellow runners. Jim leads on! I am surprised by my late-race performance!

Jim plans to stay with me until we enter the park at 36k. I continue to struggle with GI issues. While Jim is off to get me oranges, I leave the course for the toilet. I know it will affect my time but it has to happen. We have trouble connecting again but Jim finds me once he realizes I have fallen behind.

We chat a bit, he's keeping my spirits up. I never stop running, skipping water stops maintaining a pace close to 9:45, good for this late in the race but maybe not good enough. I will need to speed up once we get in the park and start the downhill portion of the race.

Jim bows out at 36k and I speed up. I feel like I am moving faster but after the race I check Garmin and it seems that my increase in speed was minimal. My legs are very tired but I am still passing my fellow runners. I concentrate on moving as quickly as possible. I am so glad this race ends in a few miles!

I cannot gauge whether I will be a sub 4, there are mile markers but I missed number 25, or this mile is going on forever. As I near mile 26 it becomes evident that a sub 4 is not going to happen. The GI issues have settled down but my tank is near empty. I pop out of the park onto Avenue Foch, I am in the last throws of the race as I see the Arc de Triomphe in the distance. I push the accelerator and move a little faster but I am at 4:00...so no PR for me. I still give it a push and cross the line at 4:01:29.

I am proud, I wondered if I would finish. I pulled off the second-best time ever! I feel better than my Chicago finish, with no muscle cramping, no nausea.

I kept moving through the hordes of runners to pick up my t-shirt, medal, and fruit. It takes me a while to meet up with the family but when we connect, they surprise me with a pastry from the famous Patisserie de Reeves.... an amazing treat for the calorie deficient!

What do I think about the Paris Marathon?

~Magnifique parcours rapide!!!! (magnificent fast course)

We had plenty of time to enjoy the streets and sights of Paris. Bob and I had arrived early and stayed in an apartment on the Left Bank, an area we had not seen before. We walked and walked and walked, that's the way to see Paris. With Jess and Jim, we spent time on the Right Bank, memorably shopping for millinery supplies! The traditional fashion supply houses offer an impressive array of feathers, ribbons, fabrics, and haberdashery. We felt transported to the turn of the century while our daughter looked through wooden cabinets and cupboards for inspiration. Of course, we spent our fair share of time familiarizing ourselves with the local cafes and patisseries, we earned it!

Chapter 7: Rotterdam Marathon

Date: April 13, 2014, 10:30am, Rotterdam, Netherlands

Weather: 52F with a 58F high for the day

Participation: 10,680 marathoners and 10,366 10K

A week later, another marathon, -feeling like a Marathon Maniac...

It was a simple train ride from Paris to Rotterdam, the second-largest city in the Netherlands. Rotterdam sits on the north bank of the Niewe Maas River. The Germans devastated it during WWII, so the city is very modern, known for its skyline and innovative new buildings. *Architectural Record* highlighted several buildings in last month's issue, so I am looking forward to seeing them in situ.

I feel better than expected. I took off so much time before Paris and then took it easy all this past week. I did lots of walking, no running, used the foam roller, and took a bath in Epsom salts...all to assist in a quick recovery from the Paris Marathon.

My good friend Tracie is also doing this marathon. It's another race known for its very fast course so we all have high expectations. We head to the start with Bob and Tracie's son, Jake. He is running the 10k which starts at 10:45 right after the marathon. Bob is our cheerleader so will spectate and cheer for Jake and then the two of them will cheer for us.

The crowds at the start line are brutal, we can't get close to our start corral. We finally weave through and arrive about five minutes before the start. We must wait until the corrals move forward to get past the fence and through the gate. We finally enter the corral and find ourselves.... last, everyone's off and running!! I am typically in the mid-pack or towards the front so we will have to pass all these people at some point, UGHH!

There are porta-potties in the start corral and since we are last, they are empty so I take advantage! Tracie kindly waits, but now we are way behind and the 10k runners are filling the corral. We hustle on.

We pass the start and join up with other runners as we head back towards our hotel. Just beyond the hotel is the famous Erasmus bridge, the only "hill" on our course and one of the famous sights of Rotterdam. I see Rem Koolhaas' building De Rotterdam, which made the cover of *Architectural Record* last month!

The course is super crowded and we are struggling to move around slower runners. We must run in stride with the others so post a 9:30 first mile. Tracie and I chat as we move along, taking in the ambiance. We hear Dutch spoken, but pick out some English so I am hoping we will get to chat with other runners?

We get a first look at the water "system." It is ingenious! Volunteers hand me a cup with a foam top, I drink through a triangular hole, there is no splashing. Toss the cup, but keep the foam top to sponge yourself!!

The course is flat, office and apartment buildings line the streets. As we head south of the bridge, the buildings get lower and trees line the streets.

Our course is a figure-eight, which we run twice; we left from City Hall, then over the Erasmus bridge for a big loop south, back over the bridge for a small loop north.

Tracie and I stay together to mile three and then run our own races. I am still trying to pass the field of runners and find a triathlete doing the same; I have my rabbit! He keeps me motivated and eases my weaving through people. He is running at 8:30/8:45 pace, perfect for me so we stay together for miles.

I hit the half (21.1k) at 1:58, great! My start was slow, so I feel like I am doing well. I wonder when the tired legs will kick in? Will I pay the price for my hard run in Paris?? The field has thinned out, and the triathlete is long gone.

I think about the upcoming miles, I will cross the bridge again and see Bob and Jake at our hotel. Bob has a bag for me with a bottle of water, Gu, and dates. I need all of it. The water stops are not happening often enough for me. The weather feels warm and I am down to one Gu. At 27k I ascend the bridge, I am over our last "hill" and I feel great. I do not see Bob, I thought I heard him yelling but missed him in the crowd. I need the water... wait!... what?... I see him amongst the crowd about a mile later! I grab my bag and laugh at my good fortune! The spectators are quite thick so I don't know how he found me. He is amazing! He tells me I am running strong and faster than expected.

The center city is fantastic. I sightsee, taking it all in. We run aside cheering spectators and pass so many city sights. The most exciting for me is architect Piet Blom's Cube Houses, a 70s residential project I wanted to see.

As we leave the city center we run past the oncoming fast runners, -I see the 3:15 pace group. There are no mile markers for this race, only kilometer markers so this feels very different. I have a homemade pace band in kilometers to manage my pace as the kilometers pass so quickly. I

seem to be doing well and decide to keep pushing myself. I focus completely on the push. My mantra is "run hard" and that is all I think about. At 30k we enter the park and it is just lovely. The weather is perfect, slightly overcast, and just a bit of breeze.

I keep it strong through the park. Soon I am at 38k and heading back into town. My pace seems fast. I have not yet posted a mile slower than 9:30, quite a surprise because typically at this point, I am struggling. I just keep thinking "run strong, stay focused, see what you can do." I know I will finish sooner than I am expected. I predicted a 4:10 but will do much better. Maybe I can come close to my Paris time. I keep pushing….

I see the Cube Houses again, still feel good. I keep pushing, the rest of the runners are going strong also. Typically, there are so many walkers late in a race, but not here. The Dutch seem to have trained for this distance, it is a race and these folks are serious. I love it, this makes me happy, I feel empowered, we all run strong!

I see writing on the road, 1,000 meters to go, how far is that?? Should I sprint? I check my watch; I am way under 4 hours, so this must be for a different race. I pick up speed, just in case. Next, I see 500 meters to go; I hit the accelerator! I can feel that we are near the finish... I am still under 4 hours; I wonder what I can pull off. I blaze on, see the finish line but also see 3:59 on my watch, SPRINT GIRL SPRINT!! 3:59:40 is my official time! One week after the Paris Marathon and I shave two minutes off my time, a sub-four, I cannot believe it! My eyes well up, a volunteer hands me a white rose and I am overwrought! I take a moment alone.

When I am ready, I move through the crowd, pick up my finish medal, hug the volunteer, and grab water as I exit for the meetup point. I cheer the finishers and look for Tracie until I see Bob and Jake. I regale Bob with my race story and earn a teary-eyed hug.

Soon we are all together sharing our race stories. Jake had an excellent 10k event. He came in 22nd overall and was the first place American! We agree to head back for showers and celebrate with a big plate of Turkish food.

Excellent race! Great celebration! I left Rotterdam with a sub-four BQ time and not a single performance regret!

Chapter 8: Antwerp 10 Miles & Marathon

Date: April 27, 2014, 9:00 am start, Antwerp, Belgium

Weather: cool 52F at the start, 66F high, sunny

Participation: 1,989 marathoners and 26,000/10K

3 marathons, 3 countries, 3 weeks.......

I'm nervous but physically I feel good. I ran Paris, Rotterdam, and now Antwerp?? Let's see if I can finish this marathon.......

Bob and I take the subway over to the race start arriving just half an hour before the gun fires. We are across the Schelde River at Linkeroever Park. The expo is set up in a large tent and it's open just in case we need to do a little pre-race shopping. We have a field of approximately 2,000 runners, so its low key, wonderful after the fiasco of Rotterdam's start! Folks are stretching out muscles, eating second breakfast, and relaxing right next to the corral entrances. The porta-potty line is not a line, just a few people! This is amazing!

Once in my start corral, I can see the big plasma screen, the gun fires confetti, the elites are off and in two minutes I am crossing the start. I see Bob to the right, throw him my arm warmers, and smile at him. The pack around the 3:59 pacer is thick but there is room to move. After 1k we circle back past the start, I see Bob again this time and toss my hat. I ditched the pace group at 2k, it's just too crowded, and it's moving too fast. I will find my pace and see how things go.

At 3.5k we start the ascent down into the Waaslandt Tunnel. The tunnel is closed to traffic until we pass through. It goes on for almost two kilometers, descending 100'! ~This will throw off the GPS on my watch!

After the tunnel, we head along the river past the center city. There are spectators, but it is low-key after Paris and Rotterdam. I run by the Steen, a medieval fort and a major tourist attraction. We stay along the river until we get to Antwerp Zuid (South) at 8.5k, where we turn and head out past the ring road. The buildings are

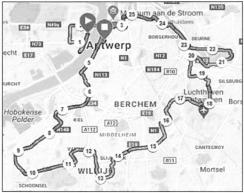

low scale, a mix of commercial and apartments, but once past the ring road, we must be in the suburbs as we start to run through leafy neighborhoods.

At 14k we are serenaded by church bells! We hear them ringing full blast until we are long past the tower. There are a few music groups along the way, funny enough most are jazz-blues combo. At 18k, I see a first, a 20-foot-tall ostrich is walking along the course cheering us on. There are no costumes on this course, so this spectator is quite memorable.

I was starting to get tired, I hit the half, 21k at 1:56, too fast, feeling too confident! I see pockets of spectators along the way. Have you noticed that my bib was printed with BROAS 474? ~an unusual name that did not deter the cheers. I loved the sound of "Brossss, hup, hup, hup." It made me miss my late Uncle Dick Broas. Why? ~Because I conceived this trip to research my 15th century Broas roots in Holland. I would not be able to share my Broas discoveries with my Uncle Dick. I wanted to tell him about my heart-breaking false start in Wessel, the wizard of an archivist I met there and the genealogy finds he led me to in Gelderland!

24k and another set of church bells toll, I am so touched by the gesture! At 26k it's still early in the race, but I start to feel that I need to back off. I drop thirty seconds off my pace and start to dread the next half. In retrospect, I should have eaten more. I ate one gel and four dates along the way. It was starting to get warm; my knee was bothering me; doubts were creeping in way too soon.

I start to realize the downside of racing in this ancient city. We run on old brick streets, then we will reach a stretch of asphalt but make a turn and we are back on brick. I can feel blisters and my ankles are getting achy.

Thank goodness I had Bob at 30k! Something to distract me, or help me regain focus? I easily see him at our designated meeting point. I stop to get my headphones, gel, and a bottle of water. All gratefully accepted and I humbly tell him I am hurting so no PR today.

I push on. Maybe it's not a sub-four, but why not finish with an excellent race time? I slip on my headphones and notice I am passing people. Is it the two gels I forced myself to eat or the cold water I am pouring over my head? As we enter Rivierenhof Park at 33k, I have my second wind. The trees give us cover from the sun and the park is just lovely. The crowd has thinned out now; I have runners around me, but the field is spread out. At 36k we pop out of the park and over the ring road. It's not as lovely here between the highway and rail yards, but I can see that we are headed for the center city.

At 41k I see the MAS history museum we ventured to yesterday in the hip warehouse district. We went to the top of the building to see the spectacular view of the Antwerp Docklands, the third-largest in the world. Better yet, I knew the finish was in hand and my time was looking good.

We ran back along the Schelde River, over more brick pavers. My excitement level was rising because I could see the Steen, then the tower of the Cathedral of Our Lady. 42k and I make the turn into the center city, the course is lined with spectators and I am pushing hard. It is glorious as I run up the blue carpet and take in the historic Grote Markt or central square. It's gorgeous, the 16th-century guildhalls, the extraordinary Town Hall and the fountain.... I finish in the medieval heart of this Flemish city to a roaring crowd! -4:05:30, a stellar performance for three in three weeks.

I pick up my well-earned medal, water, and a heat sheet. I pull my shoes off and realize my feet are just a blistering mess, but I am happy, really happy, really proud. Bob and I venture through the crowds in the Grote Markt over to the Cathedral of Our Lady for a little quiet personal reflection. I have propped myself up against the perfect photo opportunity!

The run becomes her.......

Chapter 9: Asics Stockholm Marathon

Date: May 31, 2014, noon start, Stockholm, Sweden

Weather: 66F, rain at the start, then sunny and humid

Participation: 16,000 marathoners

Heja... Heja... Heja...

Stockholm, Sweden is a city of 14 islands and 57 bridges, the Venice of the North. Floating between Lake Malaren to the east and the Baltic Sea to the west, its relationship with water is like few other places on earth. We are staying on the island of Sodermalm, in an apartment in an unusual mid-16th century wooden building. We are on a cliff overlooking Gamla Stan or the Old City, Skeppsholmen Island, Djurgardens Island with the

Royal Park that contains most of the city's cultural treasures, and the deep-water harbor. We are part of the city fabric, shopping in the local supermarkets, and preparing our meals. It has made the trip cheaper; groceries are double US prices.

The highlight of our extensive sightseeing has to be the museum that houses the Vasa, a Swedish royal warship built in 1628 that sunk on its maiden voyage, never leaving the Stockholm harbor. The perfectly preserved ship and its artifacts form one of the  most interesting small museums we have visited. My Broas ancestor crossed the Atlantic in 1634 so the Vasa was a must-see moment!

The weather had been crazy; we arrived on a day of sunshine and 71 degrees, but the next day was extremely windy, overcast, 45 degrees, and rainy. It stayed quite cool until May 31st. Race day weather seemed perfect, a cool 50 degrees and overcast. I wear shorts and a tank top. The weather was showing a little rain for 2:00 pm so I added a visor too.

What is an eating strategy for a race that starts at noon? My typical pre-race meal is oatmeal with a banana. That won't do with a noon start so I had a late breakfast of French toast and fruit, quite the rare treat.

The course is two laps around the central city with an added stretch through the parks between laps one and two. It seems an ideal way to keep runners in the prettiest parts of the city, minimize the expense of the race, decrease the number of water stations, increase the spectator's ability to see more runners, good thinking from the Swedish organizers.

Off to the metro for my free ride to the race start at the 1912 Olympic Stadium, a beautiful brick building steeped in history on the mainland. It's known for hosting more records than any other stadium in the world. I will finish inside an Olympic Stadium. ~I'm getting ahead of myself; I have 26.2 miles to run!

Just as we arrive at the Stadium it rains. A few sprinkles at first, but by race start, it is full-on rain. I leave Bob and head to my corral, feeling a bit rushed and disorganized. The race has 16,500 runners, and I am in the last corral with a 12:10 start. There is no other race, so everyone is here to run 26.2 miles. I like this, no option to quit at the half, no relay team with fresh legs at mile 20.

The gun fires and we are off, leaving the stadium to head east. Initially, the course feels crowded but we get relief as we separate at the boulevard for the first 3 kilometers.

My fellow runners seem to set a quick pace, so I try to hold myself back a bit. The rain has stopped and we now have full sun, not what I need but the sun will bring out the spectators. By 4k we are running along the water back to the center city through Ostermalm, the most expensive neighborhood in Stockholm. It retains a posh feel, this area is stunning!

The word of the day will be Heja (sounds like hay yah). We hear Heja, Heja, Heja...it means to do a cheer such as a hurrah, come on, yippee. The spectators yell it and it's on all the signs!

The course is glorious, very scenic, with lots of spectators, beautiful buildings on one side, the water and boats on the other side, and no cobbled streets.

At 5k we are heading for the island of Gamla Stan, the oldest part of the city, a must-see on all the tourist maps, home of the Royal Palace, medieval buildings, and cafés. The scenery makes the miles go by quickly.

We cross the Slussen lock to Soldermalm island and familiar ground; I ran this section on Thursday. We run along the water's edge...it is dead flat, no wind, and I feel good. I notice my first wheelchair runner. She is in a standard wheelchair and pushing herself along the course. I congratulate her, tell her I am impressed, and wish her well. At 8k we will be going up the Vasterbron bridge, the biggest climb of this race. The bridge is over a kilometer long and leads us into Kungsholmen Island. We turn right to head east again with the water on our right. Eventually, we will see the famous tower of Stockholm's City Hall.

It is warm and humid, so I start to take advantage of the showers on the course, running through them to cool down a bit. I am carrying a bottle of water, so I use the water stops to take a cup of water and dump it on my head. I do not have a good feeling about the sunny weather and try to keep as cool as possible. My pace is good, not too fast, I am holding my own.

We reach the iconic Stockholm City Hall at 11k, cross the bridge to the mainland, and turn north to Stockholm's Central Train Station. We run a series of gentle hills; I can feel

them but I shouldn't. It does not bode well for me; It's still early, too soon for negative thoughts.

By 16k we are almost back to the Olympic Stadium... ready to start the run to the parks...a little shade would be good! I expect to see Bob around the stadium, and then it occurs to me that we have not set a meeting point after the race. Nor did we firm up a plan to see each other along the course. I am losing the 5 P's as presented by my old running mentor Pete... proper planning prevents poor performance. I am getting too relaxed about these events. I will do better in Helsinki in August! I miss Bob as I run on the shady boulevard past the Olympic Stadium (he was there and missed me also).

We arrive at a field called the Gardet at 19k, and I find there is no shade. It was originally a drill field with wide-open grassy fields. It feels hot and there is no breeze to cool us. The course offers up the first bit of food, salted gherkins! I give it a try.... not my thing!

At the half, 21.1k, I clock in at 1:58:23, right on pace. I am feeling OK, not great but maybe I can sustain this level of effort longer. At the water station, the crew recognizes the flag on my bib and I hear USA, USA, USA, what a lift! It carries me for a few more kilometers over the bridge to the island of Djurgarden at 25k. We finally get some shade! The Djurgarden Royal Park is a lovely part of the course, tree-covered with more rolling hills. The park is home to many of the city's most famous museums and cultural attractions, the Vasa Museum, Gröna Lund amusement park, and Skansen Open-Air Museum. The shady rolling downhill is good but I am falling off my target pace.

As we leave the Djurgarden, we are back to repeat the course along the water in Ostermalm. I notice the beautiful Royal Dramatic Theatre. The crowds seem larger and I am looking forward to Bob at 29k. I see him perfectly poised at the Hallwyl Museum (Swedish National Museum), yah!

We are back through Gamla Stam, the Slussen lock, and into Sodermalm, this time I notice a bandstand along the river. It is filled with festooned dancers and two young men dance along with them, a sort of can-can number. It's been three hours and the dancers are still having fun!

I stop to pull out my iPod for the bridge to Kungsholmen, what a mistake! I lost almost two minutes trying to sort out the twisted mess of the earphones. I am disheartened by the bridge and the fiasco with my headphones... but I do better than most runners, I continue to run while many walked.

I am at 35k, it's Kungsholmen Island and I hear a yell from another Marathon Maniac... a Swede, Anders the Biking Viking. I give him a thumbs-up, he wishes me well, takes this photo and we run on. I love wearing this shirt because with 9,000 members in the club I always seem to find another club member with a story.

The miles start to drag and I am now in this to finish, not to garner a personal record. I am feeling drained despite my stopping for bananas at the Chiquita stations along the course. I take a two-minute toilet break at mile 24 because I have been suffering for a good portion of the second half and figured...why not?

The sun is shining on us and these later miles are hilly again. I begin to wonder, "What was I thinking signing up for a noon race? ~will this race never end!" I assumed Stockholm would have cool weather since it is so far north, but Cornwall is cooler today! My Garmin says 26 miles and I can't even see the stadium, ughh.

Finally, I see the brick building, we must circle it and then enter the stadium. I am not going to be setting any records in this Olympic Stadium but it is a joy to be inside of it! 26.9 miles per Garmin and I am so happy to be done! I search the crowds for Bob with no luck. There is loud applause so no chance I will hear his voice. I cross the finish, 4:11:20, not my best time but I've worked hard in the warm weather and am pleased.

At the finish, I see Marathon Maniac Anders again. I find out later that he has done 126 marathons and has run in all 50 US states. I haven't been to all 50 states! ~I need to think about that!!

Bob finds me as I leave the stadium and we walk to the celebration area. The marathon organizers offer the usual goody bag, along with free coffee, cinnamon rolls, foot-long hot dogs, alcohol-free beer, and bananas. There was a free pasta dinner for us the night before, too! Is this

Swedish generosity? It is very impressive. We hung out with the running crowds, enjoying the festivities until it looked like rain again.

I can't say enough about the organization of the race and the scenic beauty. It is the best marathon I have come across so far! It's well organized, well spectated, and seems well funded. It certainly deserves its billing as one of the world's most beautiful marathons.

We head back to our apartment, hoping to beat the rain and find that the day's fun continues. ~Outside our front door there is another celebration, the start of a life together, we wish them well. ~Heja, Heja, Heja!

PART II: The Maniac-24 in 12

I officially joined the Marathon Maniacs in October of 2013 by running 2 marathons within 16 days. The Marathon Maniacs are a club of runners determined to run as many marathons in a year as they can. The more marathons you run in a year, the higher level you ascend within the club. In October 2014, at the Hartford Marathon, I had jumped to level 3-Gold because I had run marathons in 9 different states or countries in one year. I felt as though I was capable of pushing myself harder, so it was time to set a new running goal. I would ascend to the highest Marathon Maniac level I could achieve in one year.

The Maniacs have nine levels, I planned to try for platinum, level eight, with a streak of 23 Marathons in 23 different US states, Countries, or Canadian Provinces within 365 days. Last year I was able to run 12 marathons in 12 months so this would double the quantity. It might sound overambitious, but I liked the idea of pushing myself to see what I could accomplish. In retrospect, it was a tough, tough year of running. Getting through the backstretch of the Istanbul Marathon still haunts me.

In Part II: The Maniac-24 in 12, I highlight my most scenic races with race reports. Several of my other races were very important to me on a personal level, and I want to mention those below:

I went back to the Philadelphia Marathon in 2014 to kick start my 24 marathons in 12 months' goal. I paced myself to match the finish time of my first marathon. I wanted to internalize the lessons I learned from my first race. I ran steady, paced myself more evenly, and finished the race feeling great, no cramping, ~like Rocky, I was vindicated!

I still hoped to successfully qualify for the Boston Marathon. I had heard great reports on a race called the California International Marathon (CIM). My fellow runners reported a terrific course, rolling downhill for 20 miles and then perfectly flat to the finish. A December race in California would mean cool weather. CIM was the perfect race for me. I delivered my first accepted Boston Marathon qualifying time, 3:56:42! I applied for the 2016 Boston Marathon. The cut-off in Boston for 2016 was 3:57:32. The Boston Athletic Association finally accepted me!

The Groundhog's Day Marathon in Grand Rapids, Michigan was of note because I completed the trail race during a blizzard. I enjoyed the challenge of the race conditions, but the airline stranded us in Grand Rapids for several days until we could get a flight out. It was even more memorable because I combined the trip with my Broas family genealogy research. The highlight of the trip was finding the Charles Broas Cabin at the Belrockton Historical Museum in Belding, Michigan. The cabin is a replica of the original 11'x14' cabin built by Charles Broas, Belding's first settler, in 1838-1839. This little gem gave me goosebumps. I stood there trying to imagine what life was like living in a one-room cabin for 50-year-old Charles, the farmer, and his wife. I stood among my forefathers!

Many people quickly attain their 100 Marathon completion by doing a Series Race, running sequential marathons in a week (7 marathons in 7 days in 7 states). I ran three marathons with a Series Race, events in Maine, New Hampshire, and Rhode Island. I ran the races on a looped course, typically a two-mile loop that we run 13 times. Much to my surprise, I got stronger as the week went on. Typically, I prefer a race with great scenic potential. I found that with a two-mile loop course I enjoyed the other participants instead of the scenery; I cheered for them! I could cheer each runner 13 times at each of three races...40 cheers each! It is a different way of enjoying a race.

The most meaningful race I did in 2015 was in my hometown of Appleton, Wisconsin. I ran in the Fox Cities Marathon in honor of my mother. She battled small cell carcinoma of the lungs and against the odds won her battle against the disease. My back bib read, "I run to honor my mother, she battled cancer and won, she showed us strength, determination, she is a conqueror." The race started on the campus of my Jr. College and finished at the park adjacent to my brother's home, where he hosted a post-race barbeque for our family and friends! Inspired by them, I ran a hard race, taking second in my age group. It was one of the best days I have had as a daughter, sister, friend, and runner.

This Marathon Maniac ran 24 marathons in 12 months and issued race reports for the nine most scenic marathons. The chart on the next page lists my marathons #18 through #41. It highlights the scenic nine in grey:

	RACE	Date	Location	Time
18	Philadelphia Marathon	23-Nov-14	Philadelphia, PA	4:17:22
19	California International Marathon	7-Dec-14	Sacramento, CA	3:56:42
20	Watchung, NJ Trail Series	3-Jan-15	Mountainside, NJ	5:03:20
21	Houston Marathon	18-Jan-15	Houston, TX	4:03:17
22	Groundhog Marathon	1-Feb-15	Grand Rapids, MI	5:08:11
23	Lincoln's Birthday Marathon	12-Feb-15	East Meadow, NY	4:32:23
24	Tokyo Marathon	22-Feb-15	Tokyo, JPN	3:57:59
25	Rock n Roll DC	14-Mar-15	Washington DC	4:45:31
26	B&A Trail Marathon	29-Mar-15	Severna Park, MD	4:09:53
27	London Marathon	26-Apr-15	London, GBR	4:08:42
28	Riga Marathon	17-May-15	Riga, LVA	4:02:07
29	Copenhagen Marathon	24-May-15	Copenhagen, DNK	4:13:15
30	ING Night Marathon Luxembourg	30-May-15	Luxembourg, LUX	4:21:17
31	The Wales Marathon	4-Jul-15	Tenby, Wales, GBR	4:20:57
32	Laugavegurinn Ultramarathon	18-Jul-15	Landmannalaugar, ISL	8:03:15
33	Mainly Marathons New England Series	24-Aug-15	Sanford, ME	4:37:38
34	Mainly Marathons New England Series	25-Aug-15	Greenfield, NH	4:45:48
35	Mainly Marathons New England Series	29-Aug-15	Coventry, RI	4:09:00
36	Fox Cities Marathon	20-Sep-15	Appleton, WI	4:12:05
37	Twin Cities Marathon	4-Oct-15	Minneapolis, MN	4:18:22
38	Freedom's Run	10-Oct-15	Harper's Ferry, WV	4:25:45
39	Marine Corp Marathon	25-Oct-15	Arlington, VA	4:22:14
40	Athens Authentic Marathon	8-Nov-15	Athens, GRC	4:29:13
41	Istanbul Marathon	15-Nov-15	Istanbul, TUR	4:27:18

Chapter 10: Tokyo Marathon

Date: February 22, 2015, Happy Birthday Steve,
9:10 am start. Tokyo, Japan

Weather: 44 F, light sprinkle at the start

Participation: 35,797 marathoners

The Day We Unite...

Bob and I are staying in Tokyo with a Boston-based run travel group, Marathon Tours. They based us at the Hyatt Regency Hotel. The race's no baggage gate is right outside my hotel lobby. My corral is one block away, so I am feeling spoiled! Corrals close at 8:45 so I head out at 8:20 fueled up on a big bowl of sticky rice and grapefruit juice.

This marathon has a new security policy, only 400 ml of commercial gel products can be brought to the race start, no liquids, no empty water bottles, no self-mixed liquid products. This policy throws me off my current approach of carrying my water and using UCan as my self-mixed nutrition. I go with the flow; do as the natives do. I will use the water stops and pray for no accidents (A man pushed me down at a water stop

in Berlin). I will use gels and my date/chia seed combo for nutrition.

~Off I go...

I get into the midpoint of my corral along with some Aussies and Japanese runners. I see very few women. Everyone is wearing lovely plastic shirts labeled Asics to stay warm and dry. I missed the giveaway at the expo, bummer! There are big-screen TVs so we can all watch the choir singing the national anthem, the start of the wheelchair race, and the shooting

69

of the confetti cannon which signals the start of our race. This race has one big mass start, but I experience no bobbing and weaving. Everyone in corral E is running my 8:45 pace.

Bob has a front-row seat at the Hyatt, 200 meters from the start. He will cheer me at another two points, just after the half and again at mile 21. The race is using kilometers, no mile markers, think metric!

The first miles are a gentle downhill as we run through the Shinjuku Station area. Cheering spectators line the streets. The area is exciting to run through, a cavern of buildings with signs covering them

just like New York's Times Square. As we move along, we hear a loud methodical beat, a rhythm, a cadence....it is the first of many folk drum groups to keep us entertained. The first 5 miles just whiz by, I am taking

in the scenery but also the dynamics of the Japanese marathoners, the steady-paced, solo runners with a steely determination. I wonder if it will be like this at mile 21?

At 8 k I notice my first of many running police

70

officers. The organizers have heightened security after the execution of two Japanese citizens by Islamic fundamentalists. Each pair of officers will run 10k while remaining alert to the surroundings.

We are now approaching the gardens surrounding the Imperial Palace. We have not toured this area, and it is lovely as we run along the moat and guard towers. At the end of the palace grounds, we see Hibiya Park, the finish of the 10k race, so I see runners crossing their finish line. There is a brass band to welcome them, along with cheering spectators. The marathoners make a turn here to run an out and back section towards Shinagawa Station.

As I settle into my pace, I see the elite men coming down the other side of the road, already back from Shinagawa station. I look forward to seeing Lauren Kleppin, the only US elite female runner and a true favorite of

mine. She has Wisconsin roots and a free spirit. After the elite pack, there are numerous clusters of team racers running together, I have not seen this in a race before. I pick out a female runner and it's... Lauren. I scream my support. She smiles! I hope it makes a difference!

At 12.5k we start to see the Tokyo Tower, like a mini Eiffel Tower, a landmark of the city, and then Zojoji Temple. It looks like we are going downhill, so I start to dread the uphill on the way back.

I notice how clean this course is, no one is dropping trash, and if they do, the volunteers quickly scoop up the bits to keep us safe from tripping hazards. The water stations are simple perfection. Each station is well marked, water cups are filled to the 1/3 mark, rather than being handed to us, they are stacked neatly with a row of cups placed close to the edge for you to easily grab.

Immediately following the water table, you find three very large bins for the cups. This setup is replicated at least five times, first five sections of Pocari Sweat drink, then five stations of water, then more stations of Pocari Sweat, then more stations of water. There is no crowding for access, cups are placed in the trash containers by most participants. The volunteers are busy yet they still cheer us on, they are all smiles, excited to be a part of the Tokyo Marathon.

15.5k and we are at Shinagawa Station, time to turn and head back. We get to cheer those behind us as we head towards Hibiya Park. I start to think about Bob, he will be cheering just after the half. It still feels like we are going downhill; I am making a terrific time.

20.5k, I am finished with the first of two out and back sections. I cross the half marathon mat at 1:57:30, perfect pacing for me, any faster and I know that I pay later in the race, any slower and I seem to come up short on a four-hour performance. I see Bob across the road in front of the Dior store as planned and we connect. I get such a boost of energy from seeing him on the course. Next, the famous Ginza corner at 21.4k and the start of another out and back section.

OMG, there is Lauren Kleppin! I see her coming back down this stretch! I scream support and get another boost of energy! This section of the race is a real highlight, famous shops line the course, and loads of energy is coming from my fellow runners and volunteers! The course is lined with spectators and they cheer, they high five, they clap. They do not carry signs, maybe they realize that a sign blocks the view of those behind and next to you, so thoughtful! This out and back section takes us to Asakusa and the famous Sensoji Temple at 29k, along the way we will catch glimpses of the Tokyo Skytree. As we race, we are entertained by more folk-dance groups, high school cheerleaders, and drum groups.

I start to settle in after the excitement of the Ginza corner, I am now into the middle miles, I am still holding a sub-9-minute pace, a good sign for a great race. I take some time to analyze my performance.... felt great at the half, seem to be holding a steady pace, I have no doubts, I know I can keep this pace for quite a while. If I can hold it to my next meet-up with Bob at mile 21/35k then I can deliver a sub-4-hour marathon. I am jet-lagged so anything close to 4 hours will be a win! For now, I just enjoy being here. 305,000 people applied to run in this marathon. I am so very

lucky; every runner is making the most of this experience. It is clear that they have trained hard and are pushing themselves, it is inspiring to be among them.

This marathon has the best porta-potties. They are perpendicular to the course at regular intervals and enclosed with barricades. The volunteers keep things organized, men have it made, easy in and out.

28k, we made it to the Sensoji Temple. Bob and I have been here three times so the territory is very familiar; I am giddy to be back again. I remember the smell of the incense, can hear the gong and the bell, see the fiery demons guarding the gate and cherish it all.

30k, a runner congratulates me at the water stop for running strong. How great is that! It is the first bit of English I hear so it comes as a great surprise. He seems to be holding a steady strong pace so I stay with him for the next 3k. He is from Chicago and got into this race through the lottery. -Like me, he is trying to complete the six majors. We arrive at a food/water station and separate. The food station has peeled bananas, bean paste buns, M&M's...a smorgasbord of goodies. Bananas = good! red beans buns = not so good! And a handful of M&M's for later!

I am running very strong and set my sights on 35k and Bob. He will be in front of the Kabuki Theater. I take time to assess my performance, 4 minutes ahead of my 4-hour pace band. I anticipate a sub-4-hour finish. I see Bob and flash four fingers. He gives me a thumbs up...

I will need everything for the last five miles. The course becomes hilly and less scenic. I expect we will see fewer spectators. Now is the time for my headphones and a marathon inspiration playlist. I ascend the first bridge feeling good, and the second bridge, still good! Two more and I start to

feel the last one, tough to keep the pace now, and I still have a few miles to go.

In the last mile, I have nothing left. I have given this run everything. I drop the pace to 9:45 and start to pray for the finish line to come soon. It will not be a sprint finish, but depending on how much further I have to go, (Garmin can vary from 26.2 to as high as 26.9 miles) it could be a 3:55-3:59 finish. I push on. A few runners have stalled at the sidelines, nursing cramped muscles. It is a push to the finish for everyone. There are spectators all along the way, so they help us to stay strong.

I turn the last corner and know that I have 200 meters to go and deliver one of my best performances....3:57:55.... second-best performance, crazy good considering my jet lag! I am welling up with tears as I cross the finish. ~So unexpected, so emotional!

We walk on to pick up our medal, shirt, and water. My calves are feeling very tight. Further on there is a booth offering a spray-on muscle relaxer. What a great idea!! I load up and let it work some magic. Further on, we walk into the Tokyo Big Sight convention center for baggage pick up, food and family meet up. As we walk into the center the

volunteers bow and meet us with a round of applause. As we walk past, they continue to applaud and congratulate us personally. This touches me and I feel a gush of emotion. I find the Japanese people to be remarkably genuine. They revere marathoners, and that respect seems to permeate the

race. I felt the support of the people of Tokyo throughout the course, and it is just as strong here at the convention center.

After baggage pick-up, we are offered a heated foot bath. I step up and drop my feet in. It's heaven, simply heaven for ten minutes. I chat with a fellow runner from Australia and another from Hamburg, both as happy with the Tokyo Marathon as I am.

Time to meet Bob and revel in the satisfaction of my accomplishment. He greets me with beautiful Japanese sweets to mark the occasion.

Later, it will be a sushi evening and a party with the Marathon Tours group on the Park Hyatt ballroom floor. The views were spectacular!

Would I do this race again? YES! It is my new favorite race. I loved the spirit of the Japanese people, the glorious sights along the way, the organization of the event. Even the weather was perfect! This is our second trip to this country and I look forward to a third.

We traveled to see the snow monkeys bathing in hot springs while staying at a traditional ryokan in Shibu, famed for its onsen or public hot baths. My weariness melted away as we shuffled from hot bath to hot bath through the snowy streets in our

kimonos and getas (wooden shoes). We took the train through the mountains to Matsumoto to see the famous castle and Takayama for the preserved traditional town and the village of Shirakawago. We finished our trip with a tour of the art island of

Naoshima, a. tiny island in the Seto Inland Sea, filled with art installations and small art museums. It was one of the best experiences of contemporary art in the world!

Chapter 11: Virgin London Marathon

Date: April 26, 2015, 10:10 am start, London, UK

Weather: Overcast, a perfect 48F at the start

Participation: 37,599 marathoners

The London Marathon humbled me!

Marathon #27, I should be a well-oiled machine, a pro, right? My performance at the London Marathon put any running confidence I may have developed over the last few months in check! But wait, I am getting ahead of myself. I am at the finish before the start, indicative of my approach to the day.

The London Marathon is special for several reasons:

First, it is one of the six races that compose the World Marathon Majors (WMM). The WMM race winners accrue points, at the end of the season the racer with the most points will take an extra $500K purse. My goal is to run all six races... Chicago, Berlin, NYC, Tokyo, London, and finally Boston. This is my WMM race #5, which leaves Boston in 2016 to finish it. The races are Gold Standard, top of the class, lots of runners (over 35,000 in London), lots of cheering spectators, a top-class elite field, beautiful courses, races that make 26.2 miles a thrill ride!

Second, my family can hop on public transportation from home and cheer for me! I like a race that is less hassle for them. There are some great opportunities to step right up to the sideline in the early miles and then again while on the Isle of Dogs and Canary Wharf. The finish area is clogged but head over to Trafalgar Square and the family meet-up is easy.

Third, the London Marathon is uniquely geared towards charity runners, last year 77% of the runners ran for a charity. This year they raised 54 million pounds, breaking the record for a single day's charity earnings for the ninth year in a row. Most London Marathon charity runners will do a marathon just once, so they make this race special. They dress up in team shirts and costumes, running for fun! ~The costumes are crazy! It is wildly entertaining to witness the "marathon parade". I saw animated characters, almost naked runners, a man with a 12' tall metal ladder

attached to his back, three men who had strapped on a race car frame, Jesus barefoot carrying a cross, a rhino, a guy carrying a dryer on his back, see the photos with a dinosaur and the police call box. I wonder how they can walk, let alone run??

Fourth, this is the 35th year and it was billed as the "Race of the Titans" with Dennis Kimetto, the world record holder vs Wilson Kipsang, the London Marathon champion and course record holder facing off. Kimetto's PR is 2:02:57 vs Kipsang at 2:03:23, both on the fast-flat Berlin course. Paula Radcliffe, the female world record holder at 2:15:25, a record set in London in 2003, is using this race as her last professional run. ~very special indeed! The best for me is another appearance by Tatyana McFadden, the unstoppable wheelchair athlete from the US. She just won the Boston Marathon six days ago and is racing again. Bob will enjoy being a spectator!

I go to this race trained to finish under four hours, I would love to post a PR and feel confident in trying for a 3:56 finish. The weather predictions all week were terrible, 100% rain all day but as luck would have it the forecast changes the night before to overcast and cool, perfect!

Bob and I will head to the start together. I will go into my green zone "Runners Only" area and he will veer off to watch the elite start in the blue zone. He will try to see me run by the Cutty Sark at mile 6.5 and then will head to the Shadwell tube stop to see me at mile 13.3. He will join up with Jess, Jim, and our new granddaughter, Josie, to watch for me at mile 21.5. We plan to connect at the finish to celebrate with an early dinner.

I arrive at my Green Zone area and the baggage trucks are starting to pull out... so it is a quick disrobe and I get my bag into the truck. I have about fifteen minutes before the race start. I am feeling quite rushed and nervous. In this race, there are three completely different start areas, the Green Zone for Celebrities and UK Good for Age runners, Blue Zone for Elites and International runners, and Red Zone for UK Fast Good for Age and Charity runners. The bulk of runners are in Red, so my Green Zone is surprisingly compact and quite removed from the rest of the crowds. It eases my nervousness and I settle down after I get in my start corral. At 10:10 the gun goes off and all three zones start simultaneously. Here is a photo from the "Battle of the Titans" Blue elite start:

~and by contrast my low-key Green Start, no stadium seating, no hot air balloons, and no spectators for the seasoned speedsters...

Two minutes after the gun goes off, I cross the start. As we run, I hear the masses yelling "hump, hump, hump" -this is not a precursor of the struggles to come but instead we cross speed bumps.... volunteers are there to flag them for us! We cross at least ten of them the first 1/2 mile. At 3/4 of a mile, we join with the elites and international runners from the Blue Start, I am met with a cacophony of boos. ~Strange dynamic but we merge and suddenly I am getting passed by quite a few runners. I am an obstacle in the path of these fast runners! Could this be the reason for all the booing?

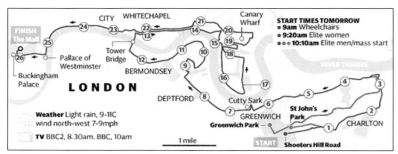

At mile 2.75 we merge again with the runners from the Red Start and there is more booing! I feel like I am humming along nicely but start to notice that I am being passed by so many runners, lots of runners, everyone is passing me. I check my pace band and look for kilometer markers, nothing posted in kilometers, only mile markers. I quickly realize that my pace band will be useless. I decide to go by feel and I feel like I am running a good but challenging marathon pace.... tally-ho, away we go!

At 6.5 miles we hit our first race highlight as we run past the grounds of the Greenwich Maritime Museum and then the famous 1869 British tea clipper ship, Cutty Sark. The crowds are huge, four or five people deep. I scan faces and quickly realize that I will not see Bob. I found out later that the police held back the spectators so one must get there early to reserve a spot. He found a spot beyond the ship, but could not pick me out.

In the next few miles, we run on a traditional English high street with shops, pubs, banks, etc., and then eventually move into a zone of low-story brick residential buildings. The spectators still line the course, particularly at the official pub zones!

I run thinking about the next race highlight, the Tower Bridge at mile 12.5. Crossing the bridge is a metaphor, halfway there, the top of the tower, the best is yet to come and for me, I know my family is on the other side of the Thames River at mile 13, so exciting! The bridge does not fail, it is amazing! ~loads of spectators, media, helicopters, cheer zones, the energy is impossible to describe. You get a sweeping view up the Thames River towards Big Ben and I start to imagine the finish. On the other side of the bridge, a view down towards Canary Wharf with its towering skyscraper's leading you to the marathon middle miles.

We turn right after the bridge and start to run facing the oncoming elite runners. I have missed the showdown between Dennis Kimetto and Wilson Kipsang. They will be almost finished now but I hope to see Paula Radcliffe. I am also scanning the crowds for Bob; he should be at mile 13.3. I am starting to feel a bit worn, nothing too severe but not as perky as I would like. The sidelines are crowded so it is tough to spot Bob which frustrates me. I learn later that I ran right by him. I was earlier than expected, posting a half time of 1:53:18, four minutes ahead of my pace band. Could this be a new PR?

As we head into the Limehouse area we turn right again and I am no longer able to see the elites. It seems Paula ran a super-fast race and I just missed her as I came over the London Bridge.

Mile 15 and we enter the Isle of Dogs running under the buildings at Canary Wharf. I like this area, there are fewer spectators, but to me, it is a really interesting part of town, with lots  of modern buildings and pockets of spectators. You have time for reflection and opportunities to interact with the crowds. I am feeling spent, so slow to a more manageable pace. I am OK for the next three miles; I break at the water stops and that seems to help me recharge.

Then at mile 18, it hits me; my calves are starting to cramp... it's that feeling you get when the muscles tighten up, first the calf muscle, then the arch of the foot. Is a charley horse inevitable?? I can try to run it out, it has worked before. I focused on seeing the family at mile 21.5 and carry on; I alternate between a slow jog and a run; it gets me to 21.5.

I scan the crowds again, so many faces, and I cannot find my family, UGHH, but then I hear "Cheryl" so I stop, turn and see no one I know. I carry on and realize I have missed them, I'm so disappointed.

The cramping gets much worst, it's all the way up my leg. I am forced to a very slow jog, alternating with a period of walking. By mile 24, I try to add in a period of stretching on the side of the course, but the well-intentioned spectators are urging me to carry on. I am reduced to yelling at my calves, slapping my hamstrings, and begging a higher power to get me to the end.

I should be excited as I see Big Ben, the London Eye, and eventually Westminster, but I greedily want to see a finish line and do not give a rip about any of the sights along the way. All I can think about is creative ways to hold off the inevitable charley horse, which will leave me writhing on the ground in agonizing pain. What 4 hours ago, was an exciting odyssey has become a miserable, humbling shuffle to the finish line. I wonder if I will enjoy marathoning again? I collect my medal, my goody bag, my checked bag, and quickly make my way to the family meet-up. Bob finds me right away and congratulates me on a BQ finish, 4:08:42... then heckles me for a crazy fast first half. -little does he know!

I wasn't the only one to find a few surprises at the London Marathon! Neither Dennis Kimetto nor Wilson Kipsang won this year. It was Eliud Kipchoge's day in 2:04:42, almost twice as fast as me! Paula Radcliffe finished 21st in 2:36:55, 1st in her age group of 40-45.

I took some time to understand what happened. Clearly, I went out too fast. I checked my splits on Garmin and I ran three miles at an 8:10 pace.... which is close to the pace I run a 10k personal best. It did not feel super-fast with all the runners passing me at the merge with the red and blue start corrals. I clearly need a pace band to help keep me in check. Running as I feel works for a half but not for a PR attempt at a marathon. I did not drink or eat enough during the race; it was cool and I did not want to take a break, so cut back on my normal intake. I spent the day before grouting the bathroom tiles. Maybe not such a good idea to be on your knees for a long time the day before the race. I am on antibiotics, which may have affected me also.

The weather was perfect and the course was terrific. I can only blame myself. I forgot the 5 "P's" ~proper planning prevents poor performance. I paid a high price for my mistakes. Five days later I can finally use self-massage and a foam roller to start to work out the painful knots in my calves.

Upon reflection you might wonder... will I do the London Marathon again? - Totally! I already checked into next year's race. It is a strange thing, but deep down I know I missed the essence of the race as I wallowed in my pain after mile 18. I need to get back there and do it justice. I need to appreciate those spectators at miles 24, 25, and 26 urging me to be strong. I can conquer this race next time!

Postscript: I came back to the race in 2016 and proudly crossed the line with 4:01:44. 2017 was a crushing 4:30:27 but I ran with an upset stomach so I was glad to make it to the finish. I missed 2018 and 2019 but was back for the 40th Virtual London Marathon as part of my 100th Marathon celebration run. I still love the race!

Chapter 12: Riga Marathon

Date: May 17, 2015, 25th Anniversary, 8:30 am start, Riga, Latvia

Weather: 48F at the start and light rain

Participants: 1,699 marathon, 4,275 half marathon

"This marathon is the same age as the renewed state of Latvia. Regardless of wealth or poverty, as a surprise or as part of the daily routine, whatever the circumstances, each year people gather in Riga to replace the usual running of errands with the collective running for pleasure... They all cross bridges and reach the finish line on the embankment. But this is not the end of the festivities... Even the winner does not feel alone here," ~Riga Marathon race guide

I come to this race with a bit of fear. My recovery from London was painful, both physically and mentally. I need to regain my confidence and my enjoyment of racing. I had no prior plan but on race day I commit myself to run with the 4-hour pace group. I feel recovered and hope that by managing my pace I can pull off a 4-hour race and enjoy it?

We are staying in Old Town Riga for a long weekend at a beautiful hotel just a few blocks from the start. One-third of the buildings in Riga are in the Art Nouveau style with funky gargoyles, maidens, animal and plant motifs decorating the building facades. It will be great fun to see them as we travel the marathon course. So much unusual architecture to look forward to!

The race starts and finishes along the Daugava River in Old Town Riga. The course is two laps and promises to take us through the highlights of Riga, all very promising! The weather is cool with very light rain ideal for running but not for spectators or photographers. The announcers are using both Latvian and English, yah! The marathon and half marathon start together. The 10k and 5k are later in the day.

As we start, we head up the Daugava River, past Riga Castle, and out beyond the large cruise ships. We turn inland to head back towards Valdemara Iela, a street we will travel four times on this course. Valdemara Iela takes us to the famous Vansu Bridge.

4 k and we start the first climb (30') on this flat course. Over the bridge is the Kipsala area, filled

with two-story wood buildings of lovely character. There are very few spectators over here but I am with a pack of 20 runners following 4-hour pacers so am staying alert and focused. The rain is light and at times nonexistent so I have overdressed. I must find Bob and shed some layers.

At 10k we go back over the Vansu Bridge again heading for the most exciting part of the course. The race directors have set up several areas of Latvian culture for us to enjoy. At 11k we experience the Culture Guard

of Honor at the Freedom Monument. We run past traditionally dressed Latvians playing the "trejdeksnis"...which I would describe as a handheld Christmas tree-shaped chime. We were encouraged to high-five and blow air kisses back to them. It was fun and I was looking forward to running past them another three times! Surprise! ~I also saw Bob and left my coat with him. I quickly caught my pace group again.

We then ran along Brīvības bulvāris and past the gold-domed Russian Orthodox Church. The Latvian Presidency sponsored a stage dedicated to choir singing at the end of the boulevard. Choir singing is another integral part of Latvian culture. They have a songfest in mid-summer with a choir of 30,000 people with a stage to hold all 30,000! Our choir was much smaller and sang songs related to famous Latvian poets, none of which I could truly appreciate.

At 12.2k we hit a turnaround point.... and the stage of the "Large

Instruments." As I ran up the street I heard and saw something like an alphorn but in brass...it must have been 10' long. In March 2015, a musician from the Latvian Symphony Orchestra showcased a trumpet six times its normal size! I felt lucky

to experience this unique Latvian entertainment. I wonder how this fascination with large instruments ever got started?

We ran back past the choir, through the Culture Guard of Honor, and then into the heart of Old Town Riga on Kalku Street with its brick paving, historic buildings, and cheering spectators. All this and it is only 14k into the race, amazing. I am feeling terrific, holding back with the 4-hour pace group, and truly enjoying myself!

The next section is an out and back along the river with the turnaround at 18.5 k. Along the way there are a few sights, the best being the old dirigible warehouse that is used for the "Central Market", a series of four buildings filled with vendors of fish, veggies,  cheese, dried fruits, meats, a truly wonderful place!

The rain starts to fall heavily as we head along the river. I am regretting the loss of my jacket as the breeze picks up and a chill sets in. I move slightly ahead of the 4-hour pace group, hoping to warm up. I take a quick toilet break and rejoin the pack. At 22k Bob magically appears offering my coat! Just the thought of it warms my heart. I never get the layering right on these cool days.

I must mention the entertaining DJs that were stationed along the course. They were a hoot, chanting for us in English, run fast, go go go, fast you go, and do not stop. It's tough to keep chanting for hours on end in the rain and they were terrific... even running alongside us later in the race.

23k, I am passing the start/finish area for my second lap and get to see the Ethiopian, Haile Tolossa smash the course record with a time of 2:12:28, the fastest marathon ever run on Latvian soil. I see it all on the big screen. He is done and I still have another 19k to go?

So now the second lap...back out past the cruise terminal and over the Vansu bridge. Along the course, you get a real feel for the architecture of

the city, a mix of beautiful Art Nouveau buildings along with the typical European mix in the old city. Elsewhere you see the two-story wooden buildings. We also pass several parks; I notice more the second time around. Here are some photos...

On another positive note, Bob found the runner tracking to be the best. Riga offered free Wi-Fi throughout the city for the day. As he logged on to the site, he could find me anywhere on the course. Just follow the bouncing ball! He would magically appear before me at random spots on the course, a spectator's dream race in sunny weather.

I hung with my pace group for the third pass of the Vansu Bridge but finally had to stop at 33k and put on my coat as the rain continued to soak us. I kept the pace group balloons in my sights through Kipsala, but as we crossed the Vanšu Bridge for the fourth time at 38k, they kept a steady pace and pulled ahead. I felt great, no cramping, no tightness, and with a coat on I was even warming up.

I carried on to enjoy the culture along Brīvības bulvāris again. Then I made my last run through Old Town to the finish.

I had the energy to run hard to the end, finishing with 4:02:07. I had fun, found personal happiness, redemption in the rain, with no pain!

The volunteers quickly hand us a medal, a finisher's bag, rain ponchos, and a white rose. I see Bob just as I leave the runners' zone.

First stop the free massage, two therapists per runner! Next up the free beer tent with no line, imagine that! It is still raining so we head back to the hotel. The 5k race started at 1:00 so by now the Old Town is

filled with celebrating runners. The Latvian running community is enjoying the fruits of their labor. Riga hosts a fabulous race and the best marathon shirt ever! ~Each year they select a Latvian artist to custom design the shirt, loved it!

Chapter 13: Copenhagen Marathon

Date: May 24, 2015, 9:30 am, Copenhagen, Denmark

Weather: low 50F at the start, sunny

Participants: 12,000 marathoners

Experience Copenhagen, Denmark Unfolds Under Your Feet....

We arrived six days before the race so plenty of time for sightseeing. Bob, Jess, Josie, and I are all staying in a big two-bedroom apartment in the residential area of Frederiksberg not far from the zoo with amazing parks and gardens. Bob and I have been out running, enjoying the spring flower display, meandering watercourses, and getting a surprise view into the new elephant enclosure at the zoo. This is our first family holiday with our darling granddaughter, nine months old now, and such a delight! Copenhagen is so baby-friendly, the National Art Gallery (SMK) had strollers for us to use while touring their facility, children's play areas are everywhere! Copenhagen strives to welcome families and it's wonderful!

The racecourse for the marathon is two laps

around Copenhagen hitting the touristed city center four times on our journey. It is a very flat course that will take us past many of the city's treasures. For me, it's a trip down this week's memory lane.

Bob and I will take the metro to the race start at Islands Brygge by the harbor and then he will meet Jess and Josie at the Copenhagen Food Hall (CPH) to graze on Danish pastries and cheer as I run by at 14k and again at 37k. Who has the better plan?? The coffee is amazing, so is the pastry, and don't get me started on the cold fermented Danish rye bread I have been eating all week. I already have a recipe to make at home!

I have been battling a sore throat all week, but on race day it seems to be gone! I feel good so will go out again with the 4-hour pace group since it worked so well in Riga. Race morning the weather is warmer than I expected so I am overdressed again. It seems like everyone running is Danish, but they all speak English. The metro or subway worked well.

This race is supposed to be 12,000 marathon runners, but it does not feel crowded. No shorter races here...just the marathon. I cross the start and see Bob right away. Note the serious-looking crowd of runners, except the crazy lady wearing the Sparta bag!

We go over Langebro Bridge to Han Christian Anderson Boulevard in the heart of the city center, passing by the Glyptotek, one of a myriad of art museums here, Tivoli Gardens amusement park, and the Radhus City Hall.

At 3k, we pass sights we toured earlier in the week; the Botanical Gardens; Rosenborg Castle, the original Royal Palace and home of the crown jewels; the SMK, where we learned to appreciate the Danish artist Vilhelm Hammershoi. We see the first water stop at 5k. There was a big group of runners packed around the first tables so I ran past. That was it, the "water stop," I had to go back! It was mad, waiting in line for water. Are they short on volunteers or lacking tables? Maybe it's an unofficial stop? I hope the next water stations are better!

We continue heading out of the touristed city center to the residential area of Osterbro. I ventured out here earlier in the week to pick up my race package at the expo. It is an area filled with five-story older residential apartment buildings and one very large urban park, Fælledparken. We hit the next water stop in Fælledparken at 8k, so crowded again!

By 10k we are at a "Broas" favorite spot, the lakes -a series of five old moats that were expanded and flooded. Beautiful apartment buildings line the lakes. The 4-mile trail around the lakes is used by runners, walkers, and strollers. We run aside one lake before turning into the residential neighborhood of Norrebro.

From there, I run back to the city center. I need to see the family and pick up my fueling "goody bag" of UCan and date/chia bars. I run by the CPH scouring the spectators but miss the family! I should have kept that goody bag; I am short on food! All those Danish pastries back there and all I have are a few Gu's in my pocket. The race offers bananas and oranges at the later water stations so I have a fueling option. Banana peels and orange rinds should bring more mayhem at the water stops!

15k and we are back at Radhus City Hall, with loads of spectators and cobbled streets. We wind our way through one of the most scenic areas of Scandinavia. We see canals with waterside restaurants, interesting shops, and plazas.

17k brings us to the small island of Christiansborg. We were here just a few days ago, a stately area that holds the Christiansborg Palace, home of the Danish Parliament, the Royal Arsenal with a sympathetic exhibit on the Danish soldiers in the Afghanistan war, the Danish Jewish Museum.... recently refurbished by Daniel Libeskind, winner of New York's World Trade Center master plan competition, and the Old Stock Exchange with the best spire in Copenhagen. It's four spiraling dragons, loved it!

It was such a thrill as we run through the cobbled streets and over huge urban plazas. The next 6k is a quiet opportunity to re-focus your race strategy. We are here too early to experience the hyperactive street life in the Meatpacking District, a hip area with restaurants, shops, and clubs in old warehouse buildings. I thought about the half waypoint. I was still with the 4-hour pace group but I would not stay with them to the finish; there's too much sun, I have too little fuel, and have spent too much time jostling at the water stations. This is not my PR course and I have the Luxembourg Night Marathon next weekend so will back off, but not yet. The pace group is enormous, 50-100 runners, so it takes concentration to avoid jostling others and tripping. I cross the 13.1k timing mat at 1:59:14.

We are running along the Port of Copenhagen. At 24k, we are at the waterside in the Christiansborg area. It's new territory as we run by the "Black Diamond" a modern theater space, then past Nyhaven, the beautiful old waterfront area, then  Ameliehaven Park, the current residence of the queen at Amalienborg Square, and up to the moats around the Citadel. I enjoyed it but lost the pace group. The crazy water stops and the jostling frustrated me, so I dropped them. The sun was draining me and I was feeling the lack of fuel.

Suddenly, out of the blue, at 27.5k, I hear Jess screaming "Mom" and see Bob running on the course with my "goodies". -Crazy, how in the world do they arbitrarily find me in this mass of 12,000 runners? I down half the bottle of UCan and start feeling much better!

At 28k we are over another bridge and back to the familiar territory of The Osterbro and Norrebro residential areas. I regret the guzzling of so much UCan. I have backed off my pace and must stop for a porta-potty along the way. Somehow, I paused my watch in Osterbro's Fælledparken so I have lost an accurate reading of my current time and distance completed which is very frustrating! I meditate for a while to settle myself, then start to wonder if I will see the family again at 37.2k? Are they relaxing with a coffee at the CPH?

I scour the faces around the CPH and much to my delight I see Jess and Josie front and center, yah! They made it; I am so excited! I stop to hug my cherub and wait for her to acknowledge me. I get that big gummy grin and then know I can move on. Josie got a few high 5's from other runners behind me while she was hanging on Mom's hip. I am on cloud 9 running

the city center, past Radhus for the last time, the Tivoli Gardens, then Glyptotek, and over the Langebro Bridge to for the last 1km to Islands Brugge.

I cross the finish so ready to be done... My watch shows 4:08 but my official time is 4:13. I lost 5 minutes while my watch was on pause. I pick up my medal and bag, then make the very slow walk to the metro dreaming of Det Rene Brod, a Danish bakery I pass daily. **Delicious!!!!!**

Chapter 14: ING Night Marathon Luxembourg

Date: Saturday, May 30, 2015 starts at 7 pm, 10th Anniversary race, Luxembourg (City), Luxembourg

Weather: 62F and sunny

Participants: 2,495 marathon, the race includes a half marathon, relay marathon, and 5K fun run

"At dusk, in the narrow streets and alleys of the old town, never-ending rows of spectators standing on both sides of the course, absolute pandemonium at Place Guillaume, the quiet green parks in the city centre, small festivals in the exclusive residential areas."
~ING Night Marathon race guide

Yes, that's right, a night marathon, 7 pm start. I will be running in the evening. By the time I finish, it will be dark, a first for me. How to eat beforehand? I went with a massive breakfast at the hotel buffet and then a roast veggie sandwich at 3 pm.

I am so excited about this race because they encouraged me to register a "Go))Go))Buddy" to run the last 2.5k with me. My buddy is Bob. The last portion of the race is uphill and this makes three marathons in two weeks, so I need all the help I can get.

Luxembourg is quite a small city, with 500,000 people. This marathon is one lap... one lap with 155 turns.... not one for a personal record, but it promises to be quite memorable. The city is spectacular. Luxembourg was one of the world's great fortified cities until its wall started to be dismantled in 1867; the Gibraltar of the North. We were so intrigued!

We are staying in the old city. I step outside and the air is filled with the festival spirit! The marathon is paired with a drum samba festival, so the plazas and pedestrian streets are thumping with music. Volunteers are handing out orange Tyrolean hats, rattles, horns, and flyers that ask for

spectators to support "our runners." At the plaza, I see a big tent with a beer bar, barbecue stand, and balloons. It's 5 pm and the party has started. In a few hours, this place will be roaring!

Bob plans to see me at 13k at 8:30 pm and again at 20k before meeting up with the other "Go))Go)) Buddy's." I should be at 39k around

11:00 pm and then we run together to finish before midnight.

This race festival offers 5k, 21k, and marathon races, plus you can run the marathon as a relay team of four. The race has several big-name sponsors, ING may have dropped the NYC Marathon but they have pulled out all the stops here, orange is everywhere. We even had a free pasta party on Friday night.

The first 5k took us through the residential area of Kirchberg with leafy, wide boulevards. A nice way to start, plenty of room to move. I plan to run this race on my own, with no pacer, no pressure, just having fun.

5k to 8k we run through the European Quarters, an area of modern buildings north of the city that is home to the EU Parliament, EU Commission, and the Court of Justice of the EU. It is also home to the MADAM Art Museum and the Philharmonic Hall.

As we cross the Alzette River Valley we get our first views of the city to the right. Once we are across the bridge the spectators are three deep! There is a bandstand set up, the drums are thundering. We see the first relay exchange at 8.8k so the course is lined with relay runners. I keep myself in check as the relay runners zoom by with fresh legs.

We are back out in a residential area of Limpertsberg for the next 4k. The area has small-scale apartment buildings, the course has lots of turns. The spectators make this area great. Imagine small groups of people cheering for us, a nice picnic spread on a folding table, bottles of wine, bread, and cheese, ~so nice. Better yet, the kids with a high five and then a big smile when you make eye contact. I try to thank as many of them as I can. What would these races be without support? ~standing for hours clapping seems harder than running the race.

13k brings us back to the city center as we enter the parks that flank the south side of the city. I scanned the crowds for Bob but there are so many people, it is impossible for me to find him in the dusky light. We run by the Villa Vauban and its lovely gardens before heading into the old city. We run the cobblestone pedestrian street of Grand Rue to the Duchal Palace, home of the Grand Duke or Monarch of Luxembourg. The photo is a sample of the center city course pre-race day, follow the arrows.

It's pandemonium as we enter Place Guillaume. The plaza is full of festivities. The big screen is rolling as are the samba drum bands. The beer tent is full. Most runners split off for the half marathon but there are marathoners to keep me company as we carry on.

We travel through Place d'Armes another ancient plaza (year 1671), more samba, more cheers, I am smiling and loving the energy in the crowd.

16k to 20k takes us out to another residential neighborhood, Belair. There were more wonderful kids, small parties, but there are fewer runners now.

I am thankful for the relay runners; they keep the energy up. I start to look forward to seeing Bob at 20k, 19.8k marks the next relay exchange, loads of cheering, and my first banana stop. I pull out of the water station and enter the park; I see Bob. He is all geared up in his running attire and "Go))Go)) Buddy" t-shirt, yah!! He laughs at my silly blue hat (a freebie at the race start), we hug, take a selfie, get organized for the meet-up at 39k, and then I am off again... through the park, past the fountain, and out for another leg in the residential area.

Over the next 7k, we weave our way through more of the local streets. The kids are still out and the small-scale parties are still going. Most cheers are in French, but I do hear a bit of English and German too. I remember one woman loudly cheering in French. She stepped out to the street, wound her arm, and yelled ALLEZ Cherie, ALLEZ...

I feel good considering how many marathons I have done. My pace is around 9:30 and I crossed the half at 2:04. I still have congestion from the cold I picked up in Copenhagen, but so far so good.

28k and we are heading to a part of the city we have not seen, the Quartier Gare. We cross the bridge over the Petrusse Valley and head by the State Savings Bank, a regal building that we see lit up every evening from our hotel room. This area seems to be more like a traditional European city, with large old buildings, grand wide boulevards... the new city of the early 1900s. Quite lovely to run through. Dusk has turned to evening and the street lighting adds to the ambiance of the race.

At 29.5k we drop down into the Petrusse Valley with wooded trails

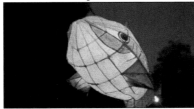

alongside a small stream, ~picturesque. I turn the corner to the park and I am overwhelmed by the Leo Light Village... Overhead, 1,000 paper lanterns light our way for several kilometers, grasshoppers, deer, snails, fish! On the ground, our path is lit by candles. We ran by helium balloons and light sculptures. It is another world down here. The valley is spectacular, folks are strolling along the course. We cross little bridges over the stream, pass by active cafés. I want to come back and stroll, it's unbelievable! At 31.5k we leave the valley and run up city streets to the Quartier Gare by the Luxembourg Train Station along the boulevard, the Avenue of Liberty.

At 35k we are back in the center city, it is a wall-to-wall party! We run through the plaza in front of our hotel. People packed in, some cheer for us, but most are enjoying the music, the beer, and a gorgeous Saturday night. We twist our way along some narrow, dimly lit cobblestone streets. It feels like it could be the late 1800s. What a great ambiance for a race!

At 37k we head back over the bridge at the Alzette Valley, ready to make our way past the European Quarter. It is quiet here; I hear the pounding feet of tired marathoners, no one is talking, heads are down. I get to meet my buddy Bob at 39k, so I am super excited. As I get to the "Go))Go))" banners, it's strangely quiet. I see Bob, standing alone but ready to roll. We laugh, hug, and then start the run-up the long hill to the finish. I needed my "Go))Go))", the last 3k was super tough. We finally get to the 42k marker and the next .2k was unbelievable! Just imagine, it's quiet and dark. But as we came up the ramp to the finish, we could hear the music, then we could see the tiki torches that lit our way into the convention center. Once inside it was crazy, disco lights, music, a mini dirigible, an announcement, we were coming in, more lights flashing, balloons, the works. Bob and I crossed hand in hand, laughing at the madness of it all.

This was the most fun running event I have ever done. I was running through parties in every city square! The enthusiasm throughout the city was contagious. Loved the race, loved the city... but the best part was finishing with my "Go))Go)) Buddy"!

Chapter 15: Laugavegur Ultra Marathon

Date: July 18, 2015, 9:05 start, 55k/34 miles, Iceland

Start/Finish: Landmannalaugar / Þórsmörk Valley

Weather: 40 F at the start, 52 F at the finish

Course Profile: total rise 6233' total fall 7200'

Why Iceland? Why the Laugavegur Trail?

Icelandair was offering free stopovers on flights between Europe and the USA. Iceland's Ring Road has been on my "must-do" list. I considered the Reykjavik Marathon but then heard about this race. The Laugavegur Trail is one of the world's ten-best hiking trails. The typical hike is four days long traveling from hut to hut. Bob and I had planned to hike it as part of our 10th Anniversary trip, but the trip never happened, so fate presented the opportunity as a foot race!

The race start is at Landmannalauger in the Fjallabak Nature Reserve in the Highlands of Iceland. It is at the edge of the Laugahraun lava field, which was formed in an eruption around the year 1477. It is known for its natural geothermal hot springs. 34 miles down the Laugavegur Trail, nestled between the glaciers Eyjafjallajökull, Mýrdalsjökull, and Tindfjallajökull is Þórsmörk, the Valley of Thor, a nature reserve in the Southern Highlands of Iceland, and our finish line.

The race offers bus service from Reykjavik to Landmannalauger, so I took the 4:30 am race bus along with most other runners. Þórsmörk is difficult to get to. It requires four-wheel drive and balloon tires, a "super jeep." Bob took a rental car 100 miles from Reykjavik to Hvosullar on the Iceland Ring Road, but to get to the race finish he parked the car and got on the "super jeep" from Hvolsvullar to Þórsmörk. The jeep went through streams and rivers before arriving at Husadular Hut, Þórsmörk, our home for a few nights in the Icelandic wilderness.

The race director advised us that the weather would be great, but the course had much more snow cover than is typical. We had to wear long tights, long sleeves, a rain/windproof jacket, head and ear coverings, gloves, gators, and trail shoes. We had to carry 500ml of water.

The bus ride out to the race start was fun. I sat next to a runner from Iceland. He ran the race last year and was out to improve his time. I learned about his father's early days as a farmer and his transition to working in the area by Landmannalauger at the hydroelectric dam. He himself was a seaman, I found his stories fascinating. We stopped for a breakfast buffet about halfway through the drive: oatmeal, fruits, bread, cheese, meats, boiled eggs, coffee & tea, the typical Icelandic breakfast.

The road was asphalt until we passed the hydroelectric dam area, and then it was rough gravel. The bus drove through the old ravines and small rivers to get us to the race start at Landmannalauger.

The weather was windy and cold, glad I had all my gear. We were warned that the volcanic highlands can be harsh and inhospitable. I left extra baggage at the lead bus (it was mandatory to leave dry clothes for the finish) which would then magically transport to the finish line.

There were three starts, 9:00, 9:05, and finally 9:10. I was in the middle group. I met several runners from Florida, one with a jacket from the Fox Cities (Appleton, Wisconsin) Marathon which was a conversation starter. I was pleased to hear all the race announcements were in English.

We were advised by the race director to go out easy. The first 10k is uphill, roughly 1500' and then the next 10k includes a flat section and then a drop. I position myself in the middle of my corral, hoping for the best. The first cut-off is at 22k, we must reach it in four hours or get pulled from the course. Being pulled from the course means they take runners back to Reykjavik, not the finish line, a disaster for me since Bob is waiting for me at the finish and we are

staying overnight at a cabin in the park. ~I have strong motivation!! I must make the cut-offs but I also want to take pictures and enjoy this majestic course and absorb every minute of this race.

STAGE 1: 12k as the crow flies, Landmannalauger to Hrafntinnusker, this section is scenic with gentle terrain but is a long climb of 1500'. The race director advised us to use 20% of our targeted time for this stage. (Garmin shows 2,703' total climb 1,361' total drop and 6.89 miles). We start with a steep walk!!!

This is a true trail and my practice runs on the Cornwall Coastal Trail serve me well. The early trail rolls up and down a lava field, we see just a bit of snow. The runners walk quickly up the hills and then run down, wisely conserving energy for the latter stages of the race. We enter an area of sulfur vents. ~ breath-taking!

We come to an area of rhyolite mountains, a rock type that creates a full spectrum of dazzling colors. Shades of red, pink, green, blue, and golden yellow make for a stunning backdrop. The snow is becoming more prevalent as we climb up in elevation. The trail is easy to maneuver. -so far so good!

At about 4k, the snow cover starts and we no longer see the colorful mountains.

The snow is slushy and once you are off the trail, the snow is a foot deep and soft, you sink into it. The drag on your feet slows you down so it becomes a single file line moving at a comfortable pace.

There are plenty of opportunities to enjoy the stunning scenery of the rhyolite hills, fumaroles, and steam vents. Iceland is one of the most dynamic volcanic regions in the world. Geothermal water is used to heat around 90% of Iceland's homes

I made it through Stage 1, the toughest part of the course. I stop at the hiker's hut which hosts our aid station for bananas, plus a toilet break, and then I am off again.

STAGE 2: Another 12k, Hrafntinnusker to Alftavatn, this is the highest part of the course, loads of deep snow. The terrain is undulating and flattens out before dropping steeply to take us down a total of 1500'. The

race director suggests using another 20% of our time here. Alftavatn is the first cut-off at four hours. (Garmin shows 1,766' climb 3,305' drop and 7.52 miles.)

The pictures from last year did not show this much snow, we need snowshoes! ~This is spectacular.

I am 14k into this ultra and I feel amazing! I cannot believe how lucky I am to be doing it. We start to see more backpackers. They cheer us on, but I think they must find us annoying as they step off the trail so we can continue which is so kind!

As we start to head down towards Lake Alftavatn (it means Swan Lake) the snow starts to decrease and I can finally run with speed. I have a cut-off to make. We can see the glaciers Torfajokyll on the left and

Myrdalsjokyll in front. There is a very steep descent down Jokultungur Pass. It's not possible to run because there is so much scree, so it's a single file walk. We make our first unbridged stream crossing...ice cold! My merino wool socks are perfect!

We see Lake Alftavatn and the aid station ahead. I am about 2 3/4 hours into the race. I had no issue making the first cut-off, but I remember that the second cut-off is more demanding so I need the buffer.

STAGE 3: The next 16k is Alftavatn to Emstrur, this section is long and flat but we have several water crossings to make. The race director suggests using 30% of our time here. Emstrur is the next cut-off at six hours. (Garmin shows 1,796' climb 2,208' drop and 11.07 miles).

At this point, I am regretting all the clothing so start to remove layers. The sun is out and the wind has died down. We are making small stream crossings and crossings over bridges. It is gorgeous scenery!

This is a photograph of the toughest stream crossing; the water is running fast and super cold. I wait my turn while the backpackers cross. The key to a stream crossing, look upstream, step side to side, never crossing your feet. I grab the rope and cross. The force of the river pulls hard on my legs but it feels good, a cooling massage!

The next section is surreal, flat, open, black obsidian sand, and pumice. We are running along a road, on a flat plain, surrounded by mountains! What a relief to be away from the snow-covered ice fields. It is not pretty in the picture, but it sure looked heavenly to me!

The runners have spread out now, I can see people in the distance. No one is passing me. I start to wonder how many will make the cutoff? I see very few runners behind me?

There it is, Emstrur. I made it in 5 1/2 hours, only half an hour before the cut-off. There is a bus waiting to scoop up the runners that miss the cut-off.

I stop for the toilet, water, and more than a few mini candy bars, coconut and chocolate have never been such a good combination before. I move off quickly compared to others that just hang out. They celebrate the fact that they can take as much time as they need now to finish. My game plan is to run this last section as easily as I need to. No worries about time, this will be a personal best so why rush? I have never run longer than five hours before, so who knows what this will be like? I feel stoked. It's fun!

STAGE 4: Emstrur to Þórsmörk, this section of the course offers some flat sections but also a few wicked hills and a few more water crossings. The race director suggests 30% of our time here, but I will take what I need. (Garmin shows 1,973' climb 2,810' drop and 10.17 miles.)

I leave the aid station with a group of other runners. It feels good to be with others, but as I stop to take pictures, I lose them and I take a while to catch back up again. This is the crossing over the river Fremi-Emstrua, the descent is steep and a rope is there to help us get down

the last few meters. I have to scale it backward. Imagine having a backpack on!

At this point I catch up with a fellow runner.... the course is sparsely populated and we are running about the same pace so we decide to stick together for as long we both can. It was a great distraction for both of us. This was his first major race. His performance is so impressive! The Icelandic are made of tough stuff! He was feeling a bit worn, so I kept him entertained and he bounced back.

This section of the course was undulating, so we agreed to walk quickly up the hills and run everything else. After a while, we caught up to others on the course and even got a few thumbs up as we overtook folks. We stopped for a quick photo session. Ahead is Kapa, the last major hill. On the other side of Kapa is the last river crossing. From the river, it's 4k to the finish.

The park area is gorgeous with yellow buttercups and blue geraniums. ~but I am ready to be across the finish. I lost my running buddy during the descent off Kapa, but I have a runner in front of me and one right behind.

My watch battery stopped 45 minutes ago so I have no idea how far it is to the finish, but I can hear a loudspeaker. I am still running, not walking! I am amazed. Finally, I see spectators, then I see Bob and the finish line. I made it in 8 hours...I started at 9:00 and finished at 5:00, wow!!

My official time: 8 hours, 3 minutes, 15 seconds....8th out of 19 in my age group. Of the roughly 400 runners that started the race, about 50 missed the cut-off. Would I do it again? -yes, yes, yes!! I was nervous until I got on the bus, but I loved this race, I felt amazing. The scenery keeps you in awe, there is much to contemplate, Mother Nature presenting one of her finest moments!

We stayed in the Þórsmörk Valley for a few days of hiking. We saw lupine meadows, mountains, waterfalls, and glacial valleys. We drove north along the Icelandic ring road as far as Jökulsárlón, or Glacier's-River-Lagoon. The icebergs in the lagoon glow a luminous blue as they drift out to sea. It is spectacular. Laugavegur Trail, the Ring Road, Jökulsárlón, it was the perfect belated 10th-anniversary trip!

Chapter 16: Freedom's Run

Date: October 10, 2015, 7:30 am, West Virginia, USA

Weather: High 61 degrees, 39 at the start, sunny

Participants: 392 start, 341 finish the marathon

"Freedom does not come easy!"

I quote the race director and mirror his words, but what an experience! Civil war history comes alive at this race. We start at the NPS Harpers Ferry Visitor Center and run a short loop to Murphy's Farm, and on the way back a deer charged through the runners. Hello, now who's fast?

After the deer encounter, I met Lisa, a first-time marathoner, nurse, and mother of three small boys. We struck up a conversation and ran the entire race together! Many thanks to her for making this such great fun.

Mile 3 and we head down into the NPS historic town of Harpers Ferry. This town was my go-to place for hiking when I was a resident of Virginia, gorgeous, historic, and well preserved. It has only gotten better!

Then over the old railroad bridge and down a flight of circular stairs to run ten flat miles enjoying the changing color of the leaves. We run the trail between the C&O Canal and the Potomac River.

Along the C&O Canal we ran by locks 34-37, then past the Antietam campground, saw some spectacular river views and leafy shady trails, sweet!

After mile 15, we start the long uphill run to Antietam Battlefield. We enter the park; the landscape changes to rolling hills and farm fields. There are numerous stone war monuments to the brigades from Ohio, Pennsylvania, etc. lining the road. We are now in the vicinity of the final attack and heading towards the observation tower and the infamous "Bloody Lane." On September 17, 1862, the twelve-hour Antietam battle injured or killed over 23,000 people, the bloodiest day in American history. This battle helped Lincoln send forth the Emancipation Proclamation. I contemplate the battle, the extreme loss of life,

114

the impact the battle had on the people, politics, and our nation as I charge up the hills.

We run by historic farmhouses purchased and restored by the NPS to

maintain the 1842 aesthetic. It is early, so there are few visitors. It's special to experience Antietam like this!

As we climb the hill to the observation tower and "bloody lane" we hear bagpipes in the distance, a stirring anthem breaks the silence. After mile 20, we pass the famous cornfield and are in the area of the park where the most horrific fighting occurred. The visitors center brings this scene to life, I am so glad we went there before the race. The white-painted Dunker Church is famous because the

German Baptist pacifists built it. It became a focal point of Union attacks early in the day. Lisa and I are still encouraging each other, looking strong, and enjoying the experience. We head away from the battlefield and into the historic town of Sharpsburg. There are fewer hills and some spectators, so the change in character is welcome (especially fewer hills).

Then it's another series of rolling hills before the downhill run into historic Shepherdstown and a finish on the 50-yard line of Rams Stadium. Lisa and I cross the finish together. I thought that my legs would not carry me this far after the Twin Cities Marathon in Minneapolis (serious calf cramps) but to cross and have this much fun, this is why we run!

We enjoy pizza at the finish line and then walk over to the after-party at the Bavarian Inn. Runners are treated to a pint of Yuengling beer in a Freedom's Run pint glass, keep the glass! There is more free food and we enjoy the beautiful view overlooking the Potomac River while watching the runners cross over the bridge into Shepherdstown. This race is a hidden gem!

In 2015, the Freedom Run coordinated weekend events with Shepherd University's 20th Annual Appalachian Heritage Festival. We went to a fabulous event featuring the gospel group Como Mamas and the bluegrass group High Ridge Ramblers. West Virginia is rich with heritage and this event packed a punch!

Chapter 17: Athens Authentic Marathon

Date: November 8, 2015, 9:00 am start, Athens, Greece

Point to Point course starting in Marathon, Greece and finishing in Athens

Weather: low 60's at the start, 70 at the finish

The Ancient Glory of Greece.....

What makes this race special is its unique history, -so, a little lesson. This race follows the historic course of the first known marathon run in 490BC. Legend states that a Greek soldier, perhaps Pheidippides, ran nonstop from the battlefield of Marathon to Athens to announce that the Athenians had defeated the Persians in a battle where they were outnumbered 2 to 1. He made his pronouncement to the Greek Assembly and collapsed, dying on the floor. This is considered the first event in uniting the Greek city-states which led to the Greek civilization we study today in art, architecture, philosophy, and politics.

When the modern Olympics began in 1896 in Athens, the organizers were looking for a new event that would recall the ancient glory of Greece. The Marathon was proposed and enthusiastically accepted. The first race was run on dirt roads between Marathon and Athens. Five countries participated, Greece, France, Hungary, Australia, and the USA. The winner was Spyridon Louis, a Greek water-carrier, in 2:58:50. He was the only Greek to win an Olympic medal that year, and in the final event became a national hero.

The 2004 Olympic Marathon was also run on the traditional route from Marathon to Athens, ending at Panathinaikos Stadium, the venue for the 1896 Summer Olympics. USA athlete Meb Keflezighi took the men's silver and Deena Kastor took women's bronze, an epic year for the US. No other marathon course has this much history, so I am thrilled to make this my 40th marathon.

The course information warns us that this is not an easy race. The first major hill starts at 10k with a 200' climb to 16k. Then we drop back down 100' before the big climb of 600' between 18k and 31k. Thank goodness we drop back down 400' between 31k and the finish.

I board a bus in Central Athens at 6:30 am to get out to the 9:00 am race start at the Marathon Stadium. We follow the course of the marathon. The natural environment is stunning but the man-made architecture is an eyesore. It doesn't seem too hilly, especially after the Freedom Run, so I relax, I should be just fine. Bob remains behind to do a bit of touring before heading out to watch me at the latter stages of the race.

The setup at the stadium is great, with loads of porta potties and runners warming up on the track. Just outside the track is the Olympic flame, very cool! I ran into the Marathon Maniacs taking a group photo and also a lovely couple that was staying at our hotel. I had almost two hours after the bus drop off so plenty of time to socialize and sightsee before the race start.

The first course landmark is the Battle of Marathon Tomb. We circumnavigate the park and can see the tombs, earthen mounds, 30' high x 150' wide containing the remains of the 192 fallen Athenian soldiers from the infamous battle in 490BC. The second mound is a tomb for the opponents.

As we move along the course, I see the permanent wooden signs designating the course and the distance traveled. There is also a permanent blue line along the road. Runners travel this course throughout the year as an "unofficial" marathon.

Our next major landmark is the runner statue at the halfway point. Runners are stopping to take pictures there, great idea!

The water stations follow the IAAF requirements, one every 2.5k. We get a bottle of water, nice! Along the way, we regularly get a cold sponge, bananas, and an electrolyte drink. The stations are well spaced and the runners are properly disposing of the bottles so no tripping hazards.

The long climb is not difficult and there is a breeze to help us stay cool. I feel good. I have no goal for a finish time so just keep a respectable pace and try to mirror those around me. The spectators yell support with Bravo, Bravo, Bravo all along the course.

I see Bob after we crest the hill at Aghia Paraskevi, 31.5k. I was not expecting him there, so he ran out and joined me for a few paces. -very cool. I found out later that his adventure to spectate was quite agonizing, so if you plan to watch the race make sure you spend time researching your plan. Running the last six miles downhill was such a godsend for me. I felt great and passed so many runners.

119

The final 2.5k builds to a crescendo as we pass the National Concert Hall, the American Embassy, the Athens Museum of Art, and then it is a left turn into the Panathenaic Stadium (built in 329BC, renovated 1829AD). The scene is unbelievable! The stadium, with its original marble seats, is unlike any other Olympic Stadium I have finished in. The proportions are perfect; the sound is amplified; the white stone is gleaming in the sun and the Greek volunteers are so friendly and supportive. It's the best medal ever! I loved this race; another one for the life list of all marathoners. I don't want to leave the stadium!

~It gets even better; my baggage pickup was right next to the Olympian Temple of Zeus. What a shot for the photo album?

Chapter 18: Vodaphone Istanbul Marathon

Date: November 15, 2015, 9 am start, Istanbul, Turkey

Race includes an 8k, 15k, and 42.2k option

Weather: 45F at the start, 57F high and sunny

"End Violence Against Women" *the theme for the 37th Running of the Vodaphone Istanbul Marathon.....*

I wake to the familiar chant of the muezzin from the Blue Mosque calling for prayers at 5:45 am. It reminds me we have come to a place that feels exotic and unfamiliar. We have been in Istanbul for a week now and have covered lots of ground, not only the must-see sights... Hagia Sophia, Topkapi Palace, The Blue Mosque but have walked the old city walls and roamed some neighborhoods that still exude the feel of old Istanbul; the Istanbul that Bob remembers from 1967. It has been a trip that has tested me. The aggressive rug salesmen are still hawking wares in the old city, and each day our neighbor next door tries to tempt us with a 35% discount on his rugs. After a few days of this banter, we smile and laugh at each other. I admire his tenacity and commitment to his trade, and he laughs to think of us Americans who have traveled so far to run in his city.

The Istanbul Marathon is unique because it starts in Asia on the other side of the Bosporus Bridge and will end in Europe on the Hippodrome at the

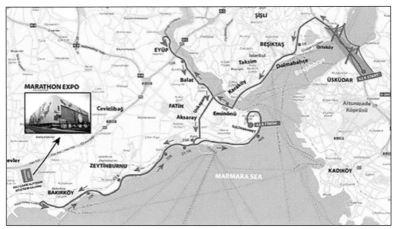

entrance to the Blue Mosque. We start the run, going over the Bosporus Bridge, a massive transportation route through the city with stunning views. It is never closed, so this opportunity to run over it is a big draw for the local population. The marathon field seems to be evenly split between international and Turkish runners, but the participation of the Turks in the shorter distance is massive! They dedicated this year's race to stopping violence against women, a bonus to my participation.

I catch the bus at 7 am right in front of Hagia Sophia, a short walk from the hotel. Bob escorts me to the bus, then I head off to the start on my own. He plans to see me at 18k and 40k. The bus ride takes us along the early 8k portion of the race, and it looks spectacular.

Off the bus at 8 am, I head for the very short toilet line and stand there until I get in at 8:50. The art of the quick in and out toilet break has not reached this far East; each user takes at least 5 minutes. It's stressful,

there are 30 people behind me in line who probably missed the 9am official start.

The 2k run over the Bosporus Bridge is worth the cost of the plane ride. The bridge takes us over the Bosporus Strait, which is the major shipping lane

for the Black Sea countries, Romania, Bulgaria, Ukraine, Russia, and Georgia. The city of Istanbul sits between Asia and Europe providing a land bridge between the Black Sea and the Marmara Sea. Istanbul is also known as the city of seven hills, each crowned with a mosque. The views up and down the Bosporus Straight with the hills and mosques framing the straight is breathtaking...

Once over the bridge we have a long downhill run that brings us to the heavily touristed more modern part of the city with the first major tourist

attraction (and the 8k race finish line), the Dolmabahce Palace. This European-style palace, built in the 1840s, was the last home of the Sultans of Turkey. The founder of the Turkish Republic, Ataturk, lived here until he died, at which point it became a museum. The private chambers, Turkish baths, harem, and mosque are all open to the public.

We pass the Istanbul Modern Art Museum and then cross over the very familiar Galata Bridge. The Galata Bridge is the major bridge over the Golden Horn, an estuary that has been the safe harbor of Istanbul through the ages. The bridge provides the connection between the "Old City" (Eminönü) and the newer city (Karaköy). The old city has the ancients, the Topkapı Palace, Gülhane Park, Hagia Sophia, Blue Mosque, the Grand Bazaar, and my personal favorite, the Spice Bazaar.

The newer city has the main pedestrian street Istiklal Avenue where you find the European style shops and the densest crowds in Istanbul, think of Piccadilly in London or Champs Elysees in Paris, or our own 5th

Avenue in NY. The Galata Bridge is the ideal place to take in the local ambiance with fishermen on the railings, extensive ferry traffic on the river, and food stalls aplenty.

At the foot of the bridge is my beloved Spice Market. Bob and I have roamed through the market three times now. I love the sprawling stands loaded with cooking paraphernalia and the mounds of spices for sale. The stands also sell Turkish sweets, nuts, and dried fruits. We have taken full advantage. Best taste of all, our daily glass of fresh-squeezed pomegranate juice, the nectar of the gods, and the one thing between me and my yearly fall cold! - Second best is Goguglia, maker of baklava and borek, a delicious savory phyllo and feta cheese snack.

My pace is good at this point and I feel much better than expected. This race is my 24th marathon in 12 months, each in a different state or country. Travel planning can often be more tiring than the races. It requires extensive research and coordination to ensure that each of these trips fulfills us. I like to find the best authentic food experiences and Bob likes to savor the fabric of the city. We both need to see the polished tourist spots but also want a feel for the life of the locals. My goal in the international races is to leave with the feeling I know the city, and the marathon is a great way to do that.

As we exit this first out and back section along the Golden Horn the 15k runners finish their race, -it has been spectacular. We marathoners still have a long way to go as we head across the city on the Ataturk Boulevard. The highlight of this section is the run under

the 4th century AD Valens Aqueduct. It spans the roadway and we run through the arches!

As we approach the Marmara Sea, we will run a very long out and back section along the coast. I see Bob just as we turn on to this stretch. I leave him the camera, let him know I am feeling great, and expect to end this race in the 4:20+ time frame. Better than I had imagined but I do miss the days of four-hour marathons, 24 marathons in 12 months has its price!

The out section is in full sun and most of the views to the sea are blocked by ugly metal corrugated fencing. We see the elite runners heading back to the Old City. I have been running with the 4:15 pace group for most of the race but as I hit the 15-mile mark I need to back off. I want to enjoy this race and the pace in this heat drains me. I am not having fun!

At 28k we finally hit the turnaround, yah! In this area, there is no more corrugated fencing and we are getting some beautiful views of the sea. So many ships are lined up to transit through the Bosphorus Strait, the sheer quantity surprises me. I imagine this is what the Panama Canal must be like. On the return, we run along the corrugated fence, with no views but it does provide some shade. I am feeling very uncomfortable, walking short stretches, I will get there eventually! I realize that 24 marathons in 12 months is my top limit, I have moved into the "This is NOT fun" place. I need another spark to perk up my attitude!

I see Bob at 40k, it's a relief to know that I am on the home stretch! I start to revel in the accomplishment of this year, so many miles, so many exotic races. My goal as a young woman was one marathon. I never imagined I could do something like this.

Soon I round the corner and enter Gulhane Park at the foot of Topkapi Palace. The park is the home to a flock of parrots and their merry mocking calls resonate through the trees as we

start the last small hill climb up to the Old City.

Then we run along the tram tracks at the base of the Topkapi Palace walls. Bob and I spent a day sightseeing inside the palace. Among the treasures, we saw the 86 carat Spoonmaker's diamond, the rod of Moses (which I had to go back to inspect twice), Abraham's saucepan, John the Baptist's hand, and Mohammed's footprint in stone. They have an unbelievable collection of religious relics.

The crowds amass as we enter the Hippodrome for the last hundred meters. The Hippodrome is now a plaza, but I imagine it as the chariot race track it once was and take my running up a notch for the push to the finish. I post a time of 4:27.

We loved this trip. Istanbul is a city that attempts to walk the line between ancient and modern. It can claim the glories of Constantine with his Byzantine empire and Christian faith, then there is the great Ottoman

Empire with its Muslim faith and Ataturk, founder of the modern Turkish Republic. This dueling heritage makes for a unique glimpse into another culture.

Stretching along the Golden Horn to the Sea of Marmara, the fortified walls of Istanbul were built to protect the city from the early Byzantine period to the fifteenth century. We ventured to the far western side of the city to see the walls, not an easy mission using public transportation, but the experience was priceless. Step back in time, open your mind and who knows what will happen...

Crazy stuff happens! Istanbul has had a large feral dog population since before the Ottoman Empire but has recently come under pressure to eradicate the dogs. They are not typically kept as pets here. They are seen as an undesirable part of the urban fabric. Bob and I were joined by a feral dog on an early morning run by Topkapi Palace. I was nervous as he ran alongside us and nipped at any of the other dogs that tried to join in. -but his demeanor quickly conveyed his joyful desire to run with our pack and show his fellow mutts that he was indeed an alpha.

Later, we learned that because of citizen pressure, the city has undertaken a program to pick up each dog, provide inoculations, neuter/spay and then release the dogs back to the location of pick up. Each local dog has an ear tag to show participation in the program. This is so much better than the original plan of releasing them in the already overpopulated forests outside of Istanbul. Explore, keep an open mind and you might make a new friend... furry or not!

Part III: The Speedster-Finding My Inner Rabbit

I decided, after finishing Istanbul, that 24 marathons in 12 months would not be a personal record I wanted to break. I was happy with the Platinum level of the Marathon Maniac club and would not pursue the top level of Titanium. That level requires 30 marathons in different US states or 20 countries in a year. The combination of running two marathons a month and pushing myself to be fast was physically draining. Travel planning was no longer enjoyable. It was time to regroup, refocus, and find a new goal for my running. I decided to commit myself to weekly speed sessions and focus on getting faster.

I chose to run fewer marathons and picked faster courses, hoping to pick up BQ finish times. My trip back to LA for a sub-four finish was a bust. The race day temperature rose to 88 degrees. I am a winter-born baby from the cold state of Wisconsin so melt in the heat.

Five weeks after the LA Marathon, I would test my speed again at the Two Rivers Marathon in Pennsylvania. The course is rolling downhill for the first half, the second half is almost flat as it follows the Delaware River. I had a spectacular run. It was the perfect mix of cold weather, a downhill asphalt course through woodlands, and a long flat finish. I took first place in my age group and won the Grand Master category at the RRCA Pennsylvania State Championship, which was a part of this event. I returned in 2017 and 2018 posting great times each year.

In 2016, I found my wheels at marathons in London, New York City, and Rehoboth Beach. In 2017 I focused my speed on downhill courses where I shine, so back to Two Rivers, the Glacier Marathon in Austria, and Leading Ladies in South Dakota. Not only did I get faster, but I jumped to the 55-59 category so I would only need a sub 4:05 as a Boston qualifying time. I was winning age group awards regularly at races. In 2018 I discovered the Revel races, a series of downhill races typically run in the mountains. I did well and hoped to try more races in the series. I was regularly posting sub-four-hour marathon finish times in 2016 and 2017.

It wasn't all about speed. I tried my first race in a National Park at the Crater Lake Rim Run and found my piece of running heaven. In October of 2016 a group of us went to the Grand Circle Trailfest for three days of trail runs in Bryce, Zion, and the Grand Canyon National Parks; ~loved it! I started to seek out races in National Park like settings which lead me to some spectacular places; the Cotswold Way in England for Race to the Tower, the Austrian Alps for the Pitztal Glacier Marathon, the Spearfish Canyon Scenic Byway in South Dakota for the Leading Ladies Marathon and the Petrified Forest Marathon in Arizona.

The Bataan Death March was not in White Sands National Park; it was on the high desert terrain of the adjacent missile range. The scenery was terrific but I chose this race because it is conducted in honor of the heroic service members who defended the Philippine Islands during World War II, sacrificing their freedom, health, and, for some, their lives. I was able to shake hands with some of the last living survivors of the Bataan Death March in the Philippines before the start of the race. I have a very distant relative that survived the Bataan Death March, so much to contemplate!

I would complete my quest to run each of the marathon majors. "The Abbott World Marathon Majors is a series of six of the largest and most renowned marathons in the world which form an annual series to determine the world's best male and female marathon runners." I received my Six Star Finisher certificate and medal after completing my final major, the 2016 Boston Marathon; my name is in their Hall of Fame.

In 2016, I went to the Vermont City Marathon. It was the hottest day on record there. I wisely started my race slow and steady. At mile 21 (four hours after the start) the race organizers canceled the race, the wet-bulb temperature exceeded 82 degrees. I continued with a slow jog to cross the finish line at 4:51:30. Anyone that finished the race with a time slower than 4:30 was not awarded an official time. I identify the race as #45 ½ in my mental list of 100 ½ marathons but have not included it in my official 100 marathon list.

With a focus on speed, I ran thirty-one (and a half) races in 27 months posting some great race times. I found my inner rabbit. The chart on the next page sequentially lists my marathons #42 to #72. I distributed eight race reports from a cross-section of the races, typically a mix of an unusual setting and personal hardship. I highlight the eight race reports in grey:

	RACE	Date	Location	Time
42	LA Marathon	14-Feb-16	Los Angelas, CA	4:17:17
43	Two Rivers Marathon	26-Mar-16	Lackawaxen, PA	3:51:52
44	Boston Marathon	18-Apr-16	Boston, MA	4:23:46
45	London Marathon	24-Apr-16	London, GBR	4:01:44
46	Bay of Fundy Marathon	26-Jun-16	Lubec, ME	4:20:56
47	Crater Lake Rim Run	13-Aug-16	Crater Lake, OR	4:39:25
48	Tallinn Marathon	11-Sep-16	Tallinn, EST	4:17:42
49	Oslo Marathon	17-Sep-16	Oslo, NOR	4:13:05
50	New York City Marathon	6-Nov-16	New York, NY	4:01:31
51	Rehoboth Beach Marathon	3-Dec-16	Rehoboth Beach, DE	3:56:17
52	Bermuda Marathon	15-Jan-17	Hamilton, BMU	4:26:10
53	Hilton Head Marathon	11-Feb-17	Hilton Head, SC	4:21:08
54	Bataan Memorial Death March	19-Mar-17	White Sand, NMs	5:05:23
55	Two Rivers Marathon	25-Mar-17	Lackawaxne, PA	3:54:10
56	Boston Marathon	17-Apr-17	Boston, MA	4:19:47
57	London Marathon	23-Apr-17	London, GBR	4:30:27
58	Kigali International Peace Marathon	21-May-17	Kigali, RWA	4:36:56
59	Race to the Tower Day 1	10-Jun-17	Stroud, GBR	6:04:42
60	Race to the Tower Day 2	11-Jun-17	Cheltenham, GBR	6:03:45
61	Pitztal Gletschermarathon	2-Jul-17	Imst, AUT	3:53:29
62	Leading Ladies Marathon	20-Aug-17	Spearfish, SD	3:56:20

	RACE	Date	Location	Time
63	Nebraska State Fair Marathon	26-Aug-17	Grand Island, NE	4:28:03
64	Beyond the Beach	17-Sep-17	Gary, IN	4:51:15
65	Petrified Forest Marathon	21-Oct-17	Holbrooke, AZ	4:23:02
66	New York Marathon	5-Nov-17	New York, NY	4:06:13
67	Firenze Marathon	26-Nov-17	Florence, ITA	4:22:35
68	Bahamas Marathon	13-Jan-18	Nassau, BAH	4:48:00
69	A1A Marathon	18-Feb-18	Fort Lauderdale, FL	4:30:24
70	Two Rivers Marathon	24-Mar-18	Lackawaxen, PA	3:55:44
71	Boston Marathon	16-Apr-18	Boston, MA	4:09:40
72	Revel Mount Charleston	28-Apr-18	Las Vegas, NV	3:55:11

Chapter 19: Bay of Fundy Marathon

Date: June 26, 2016, 7:10am start, Lubec, Maine

Weather: 54F at the start, high of 72F

Participants: 209 marathon finishers

May the Course Be With You.....

Lubec, Maine is the easternmost town in the US. It sits at the upper northeast corner of Maine. I was interested in running in the cool summer weather. I signed up for the race before I discovered its real appeal; the area is made famous by the adjacent Campobello Island, the Canadian summer home of our 32nd President, Franklin Roosevelt, and his family. How do you start a race in the US, run 20 miles in Canada, and finish in the US? It's a homeland security nightmare!

The town of Lubec is quite small, pop. 1,359. The race allows 350 runners for the marathon, 350 for the half marathon, and they also offer a 10K and a mile fun run. Runners overtake the town and the residents love it! This sign into town says "Lubec: Home of the Bay of Fundy Marathon." Campobello Island is even less dense, with a population of 1,056. Between the race volunteers and the course spectators, it seems everyone participates in the event and the enthusiasm is contagious!

The marathon starts at the West Quoddy Head lighthouse, 5.5 miles outside of town while the half marathon starts on Campobello Island.

From the local school, they bus us to the start line. It is a small-town race with plenty of facilities and free coffee, ~nice! This race offers an early start option for race walkers, so we see many of them as we head out to the lighthouse.

The scenery at the lighthouse is idyllic but the runners are all talking about one thing... the hills on the course! Rolling hills have a different definition in Maine! The race director warns us, "the early part of the race, the first six miles back to Lubec is pretty flat, Campobello Island is more challenging, start easy." I hear a few gasps but we drove the course yesterday so I know what I am in for. I had always planned to enjoy this course, no PR on my mind, a 26.2-mile scenic ride!

We are off, running rolling hills with a gentle downhill so my pace is strong. I battled a severe chest cold earlier in the month and then plantar fasciitis, but it is all behind me now. 5.5 miles into it and I see Bob cheering in Lubec, I feel fantastic so give him a thumbs up.

Next, we will cross the FDR Memorial Bridge into Canada, run through border control, and then the real hills start. Yesterday we had to visit both the Canadian and US passport control, present our passports and declare that we were participants in the race. Our race bibs have been electronically processed so that we can automatically pass through passport control without stopping. How cool is that!

After crossing the bridge to Campobello Island, the course will take us past the Roosevelt

Campobello International Park, the summer retreat of the Roosevelt's, and a lovely park that offers tours of his home and some of the nicest coastal and forest walks in the area. Then past the adjacent Herring Cove Provincial Park, the site of the previous days' pasta party and lobster bake. Out to the small town of Wilson's Beach and onward to the Head Harbor Lighthouse where we turn around and come right back to Lubec for our finish.

I settle in and enjoy the race, I am feeling remarkably good, keeping a

steady pace and thanking the spectators along the way. My fellow runners do not seem much like chatting. It is the hottest day of the year in Maine, with full sun and 68 degrees.

We run by beautiful coves...

and over plenty of long hills...

and through Wilson's Beach (O' Canada):

and then to mile 16 and the turnaround at Head Harbor Lighthouse. This lighthouse is only accessible to the public at low tide! ~To walk out to the lighthouse, you descend a metal stair down to a stone beach... back up a set of stairs, onto another "island" over a bridge, then down another set of stairs to another beach, back up again and over to the lighthouse. What fun!

Heading back to Lubec, I lost my rabbits, or fellow runners... two men I played cat and mouse with most of the way out. I would lead downhill and they would lead uphill. Eventually, I caught up to several women, so had some company, a gal doing her first marathon and another fellow Marathon Maniac.

The race support was amazing, some aid station volunteers dressed as Hawaiian dancers. We saw random signs along the course, for example, this gem at the local school, "MAY THE COURSE BE WITH YOU!"

Miles 19 – 22 were a relentless uphill, miles 22- 24 more uphill. I did a bit of walking to crest the last hill at mile 25 but finally saw the bridge back to the good old USA. I finished with a sprint. Finish time 4:20:26 and 6/23 women ages 50-59. I was quite pleased!

The post-race celebration was terrific. The race tent offered homemade soup, locally made yogurt with real maple syrup, frozen Maine wild blueberries, and the traditional bagels, fruit, and water. The awards were all handmade by a local potter. The medals are always local, handcrafted from pewter. This year we received a starfish. Medals from years past include sea urchins, scallop, and sand dollars. The town had a street party with access to a craft brewer, home-baked food, artisan wares, and crafts.

~no post-race ice bath was required; the water was 45 degrees!

Great organization by the race director, beautiful course, cool weather, and full support from the community. I feel like I was part of a big event, yet it had all the intimate qualities of a small race. I loved it, hills and all! From the race bags (fisherman's bait bags) to the craft brewer in town (yah, they ran out of beer, it was so popular after the race) this race rocked every detail.

We stayed the week and brought the kayaks along to test the waters in Cobscook Bay State Park. It's known for its rugged tidal beauty and rocky shores. Tide changes here average 24 feet, with some ebbing and flowing 28 feet. Cobscook is derived from a Maliseet-Passamaquoddy word for boiling waters. We went out for a scouting hike around the bay to watch the rapid tidal changes, rapids emerged as the bay started to drain to the ocean. This is an area where you must know your tide's schedule!

Back in Lubec, our favorite sight was the McCurdy's Smokehouse, an old herring processor. The business closed in 1991, and the structures were added to the National Register of Historic Places in 1993. Since then, some of the buildings were repurposed as a waterfront museum to the historic trade. Inside the building, we saw the rooms where herrings were deboned, smoked, pickled, and prepped for shipping. Some locals say that the scent of brine still lingers in the buildings, but we were surprised by the ever-present smell of smoke.

Campobello Island, lighthouses, kayaks, and hiking, you can stage an active recovery after enjoying the Bay of Fundy Marathon. It's a small-town wonderland!

Chapter 20: Crater Lake Rim Run

Date: August 13, 2016; 7:30 am, Crater Lake, Oregon

Weather: Sunny, 67F, 88F at noon, 100F by 5 pm.

Participation: 90 marathon, 167/half, 158/quarter

Altitude: 5,980'-7,840'; elevation gain of 2,422'

Snug and low

Rimmed by your mountains

crowned with snow.

Your phantom ship sails waters blue

Your sloping brow fir-scented drew

An island set where hemlocks strewn

Mid flowering plants and trails rock-hewn

The winds that whisper along your shore

Could tell a thousand tales or more

And I a pygmy, dwarfed beside

Can see the Creator's loving hand abide.

Crater Lake–by Maurice R. Keep

I required Oregon for my 50-state quest and this was Julia's choice as the most scenic race in her new home state of Oregon. It was my first run in a National Park. I can't imagine a more spectacular place to run a marathon! Bob and I flew to Portland for a few days' visit before the two couples made the four-hour drive to Crater Lake. Great scenery along the way and an iconic stop in Eugene aka "Tracktown, USA" for a vegetarian lunch and a chance to take in the atmosphere.

We came into Crater Lake via the North Entrance, hoping to see how bad the recent fires had been. We could smell the smoke and see some scorched trees along the road. In early August the Bybee Fire burned its way to Crater Lake, close to our race start. Evacuation warnings ordered by the National Park Service were lifted five days ago. The air was clear and there was only minimal damage visible from the Rim Road around Crater Lake. After a coffee and some more sightseeing, we left the park to spend the night in Klamath Falls, the closest town to the main park entrance.

Race morning, we went back to Rim Village to park and catch the race bus to the start at the foot of The Watchman, an isolated summit that has a superb view of Wizard Island.

We ran the race on asphalt except for the first few miles which were being repaved and the last four miles which were on a pumice trail. There were very few cars or spectators, but with views of Crater Lake, we will keep our spirits soaring.

We are off and running on West Rim Drive towards the Devil's Backbone, an unusual wall of vertical dark rock. Julia and Shane ran together and Bob positioned himself towards the back of the pack. Bob and I had

concerns about running at such a high altitude, 5,980' to 7,840', but so far so good. We pass by the road to the North entrance, and then Llao Rock, another summit that blocks our view of the lake.

3 miles, we are almost halfway to Bob's 6.7-mile finish at Cleetwood Cove. The cove is the departure point for the boat tours on Crater Lake. It's the only place to access the lakeshore.

Bob's finish time was 1:20:40, a first-place finish in his age group! While he is recovering at the finish line, I was rewarded with gorgeous views over the next few miles. Bob took the race bus to Lost Creek, our marathon finish.

Bob grinned as he rode past me groaning up the notorious hill, notorious for its 4% grade from mile 9 to mile 14 ½ and its 1900' drop from mile 14 ½ to mile 22.

141

My immediate goal was Cloudcap overlook so up and up and up I go. Cloudcap is the highest overlook on the rim, 7,865' in elevation and 1,690' above the lake. I have plenty of time to anticipate the view on the way up. Crater Lake is nearly 900' below me, and the

opposite rim of the crater is six miles away. At 1900' deep, Crater Lake is the deepest lake in the United States. Scientists consider Crater Lake to be the cleanest and clearest large body of water in the world.

It's a long climb and some walk breaks had to happen! But I arrive at the turnaround and the glorious downhill starts! I planned to run for as long and as fast as I could to take advantage of the

downhill gift. As I reached the end of this one mile out and back section, I see Julia! She is all smiles and we stop for a hug and a photo.

Shortly after our meet up my running watch stopped working! Panic and deep frustration set in. Was it the watch battery? Was it the bad satellite reception or an end-of-watch life event? I could not get it restarted so no choice but to run by feel. We will see what the day brings!

I raced down the hill stopping for just one breathtaking photo of what they call the Phantom Ship. It looks so small out on the water but is 165' tall. It was the last great water view we had since the course started to turn south away from the lake to head over to the Lost Creek Campground and the marathon finish. (See photo on the next page)

The course held one more surprise for us, another uphill climb of almost 800' between miles 22 and 24! The steepest climb of the race. After all,

the downhill running my legs were screaming up the hill, I had to run/walk it and even did a bit of walking on the downhill!

As we hit the campground, we started to hear the unfamiliar sound of people cheering for us, ~awesome! I crossed the finish line in 4:39:25, #35 out of 90 runners, 8 out of 27 women, and took 2nd place in my age group. I hung out at the finish line taking advantage of the shade and the little stream next to the food tent as the temperatures climbed to 90 degrees! Here is a shot of Julia and Shane sprinting to the finish line:

The four of us took the bus back to Rim Village. After a wash-up, quick change, and grazing, we were on our way back to Portland for the next phase of our adventure, the Columbia Gorge, and a stay at the Timberline Lodge on Mount Hood.

I loved running in Crater Lake National Park and if I can find a marathon in another National Park, it will be on my bucket list of races!

Timberline Lodge at Mount Hood stands next to the Pacific Crest Trail, so I had to go for a run! The views from the trail were extraordinary!

.

A short two-hour car ride took us to the Oregon coast. Here is a final photo from the Cascade Head trail near Neskowin, Oregon.

Chapter 21: Tallinn Marathon

Date: September 11, 2016, 9:00 am, Tallinn, Estonia

Weather: start 55F, high 70F, sunny

Participants: 1776 marathon finishers

An Estonian Proverb, *"The work will teach the maker – töö õpetab tegijat"*...

Tallinn's Old Town is a UNESCO Heritage Site, it consists of an upper walled town which was the area for the leaders of the town and the wealthy upper class. The walled lower town was the Hanseatic merchant area filled with Germans, Swedes, and Dutch traders. Tallinn's city walls and towers are some of the best-preserved in all of Europe so that urban plan along with the lovely alleyways, cobbled streets, and ancient buildings make this a spectacular place to visit. Tallinn, Estonia sits on the Gulf of Finland of the Baltic Sea. Many tourists come here on a cruise taking in St. Petersburg, Helsinki & Stockholm. It is also supposed to be a great place for bridal hen parties? We were fortunate to be in Tallinn during a week-long arts festival and stumbled upon some great events....my favorite was a small concert at the Carved Stone Museum!

The Tallinn Marathon is a weekend running festival, it starts with a youth 5k on Friday evening. The race had a big turnout of young people. We cheered the race while in Freedom Square and the winner, Andi Noot, sailed through the finish looking very  relaxed, giving high fives to spectators along the way. He finished in 13:31 just 15 seconds off the Estonian 5k record, crazy fast in my book. This is a photo of the start in Freedom Square, all the white shirts are runners warming up with the folks on stage.

Saturday morning was the 10k, Bob followed the route during his morning run. Some might call that a bandit run! He passed lots of walkers and saw an area of the city that we never got to with lovely wooden houses reminiscent of the homes in Riga, Latvia. Children's races fill the afternoon at Freedom Square.

Sunday is the Marathon with a 9:00 am start and a half marathon at noon. Both courses cover the same territory, but the marathoners run the route twice. The race starts on the edge of the old city in Freedom Square, so we booked a studio apartment in the heart of Old Town for the weekend. The apartment was in a Hanseatic merchant's house dating from 1466. We had to walk through a covered portico to a courtyard and up a tiny winding stone stairwell to get up to our unique apartment, ~glorious!

The marathon is much smaller than I had expected, 2,100 people signed up but only 1783 finished. There were only three American women and one was Marathon Maniac-Marathon Globetrotter Liz,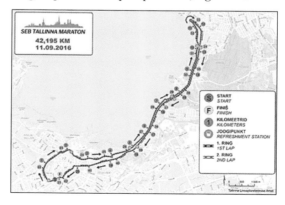

who is currently living in Egypt. She had on her pink Marathon Maniac diva shirt, so was very easy to spot in the crowd. A quick chat and we were off to the race start. Most of the runners are Estonian or Finnish, there are decidedly more men running but plenty of women too. The Estonian triplets (Leila, Liina & Lily, the trio of Rio) that just ran the women's Olympic marathon did a dance and a cheer for us before the start gun went off.

The first mile we climb a gentle 75 feet and then descend to the waterfront, we run outside Old Town along a park, the railroad station, and past the famous Fat Margaret's Tower. I was expecting some cobblestone streets, but we ran on asphalt, -terrific. I run a good portion of the early race with an Englishman who is a member of the 100 Marathons Club. It is always fun to meet new people along the course! I will see Bob again at 5.5k or 3 miles. Miles 3 to 11 are on the waterfront.

Bob hopped the tram and got to the park along the waterfront to take this amazing photo.

Once out of the park we ran on the Pirita Promenade for 2k. We had the Baltic Sea on one side and the Maarjamae Memorial on the other. The memorial is a concrete obelisk almost 100 feet tall. Our next landmark was the Tallinn TV Tower. We continued along the Baltic Sea for another 4k then looped back to run the same path back to the center city.

I loved the smell of the salty sea; the breeze brought the scent our way at several spots along the course. We got glimpses of the sandy shore, the boat marinas, and wooded areas along the coast. We also saw the elite runners coming back towards the city center, two Kenyans in the lead but an Estonian runner not far behind.

We could see the cruise ships out in the harbor. The terminal sits right at the base of the Old Town, fantastic for the hordes of tourists that come via the cruise lines.

I see Bob again at 18k/mile 11 just before we are heading back to the city center, at this point I have fallen slightly behind the 4-hour pace group, the coastline provides no shade so the heat is starting to bother me.

We run through Kalamaja, which is the bohemian side of Tallinn with lovely colorful wooden homes. They are highly valued here and are now being preserved.

I make a loop around the old city center back to Freedom Square, halfway, 13.1 miles in two-hours. I am not feeling chipper, so I back off a bit for the second loop. I take full advantage of the water stations. Every station had Vichy water, electrolyte drinks, bananas, raisins, brownies, salt, and sugar. ~Bowls of salt and sugar, a first in my running career.

Along the course, I heard an accordion, I saw a group of mimes and several sets of cheerleaders. One set of cheerleaders had a boom box playing "Born in the USA"! There were not too many spectators but those we had sometimes called out my name "Shear ill" or go USA or haup, haup, haup or go, go, go! I see Bob again at 27k/17 miles.

On the second loop, I see more of the runners. By the time I see Bob at 39k/24 miles, I had already witnessed a continuous parade of half marathoners running up the path next to us.

I am passed by the lead half-marathon runner, a Kenyan at 38k. I try giving it a good push for a short while in his honor. The lead female passes me at about 41k!

I finished and it was not easy! It seemed to be much harder than I thought it would be, perhaps the heat and humidity. Maybe I am not as fit as I thought? The work will teach the worker – *töö õpetab tegijat*, an old Estonian proverb to teach me a lesson.....

I hope I improve for my race in Oslo next weekend. This course was flat and had very few turns, so it's ideal for a speedy race. My fancy new watch shows a distance of 26.7 miles. I was expecting a more accurate 26.2 and a finish time of 4:12 rather than my 4:17:42. I was 4th of 18 runners in my age group, which is consoling.

The race medal is beautifully done, they gave us a great Nike race shirt in black and there was an amazing spread of food for the marathoners, red pasta with chicken & veggies, wraps, salads, doughnuts, pastries, soup, pieces of bread, first-class!

The race was well done; it was not my best performance, but all races cannot be my best. I earned my second flag with the Marathon Globetrotters; this is my 20th country completed!

If you have the chance, run one of these events and see this spectacular Baltic city. Bob and I have five days of relaxation in Bergen with the family and then we are off to the Oslo Marathon, ~tally ho!

Chapter 22: Oslo Marathon

Date: September 17, 2016, 9:20 am start, Oslo, Norway

Weather: Overcast, low 60's start, sunny 70F finish.

Participants include 2,500 marathoners, 10,000 half marathoners, 6,000 10k runners, 50 Oslo Triple runners. My country count #21

Å få blod på tannen; translation, to get blood on your tooth; meaning, to become inspired and driven to do something...

My mother's ancestors came from Norway so we have been hoping to see our home country. Her photo journal sold us on it several years ago. Fjords, ocean views, scenic train rides, and remote mountain villages won us over. We convinced the family to join us in Bergen, a gorgeous city that sits in the Fjords. We stayed just up the hill from the historic warehouses that line the waterfront. It was a child-friendly city with a great aquarium that our granddaughter adored.

Bob and I left the family to take the Norway in a Nutshell, train-boat-train trip from Bergen to Oslo. It is a spectacular day-long journey. First, we catch a scenic train to Voss on the Bergen Railway. From Voss, we travel by bus through charming villages, scenic nature landscapes to catch a fjord cruise on the Aurlandsfjord and the on the narrow Nærøyfjord which is on UNESCO's World Heritage List. Unfortunately, the clouds hung low so our fjord trip was spent looking at a tv screen imagining what could have been... We arrived in the small village of Flåm, where we catch the legendary Flåm Scenic Railway through the fjords. The views down the fjords were spectacular, stunning waterfalls drop from the cliffs. The last leg is the train to Oslo through the mountains. What a day!

On Friday afternoon Bob and I met up with Gry, a NewRo Runner friend that has moved back to Norway. She is running the half on Saturday so we go to the race expo to get our race bibs and soak in the atmosphere before heading to her place for pasta dinner and a catch-up. We reveled in the excitement of the race and I learned more about Norway, sweet!

Those with the stamina sign up for the Oslo Triple. They must finish the marathon in under 4:30 so that at 1:30 pm they can join the half marathoners at the start line. They must finish the half under 2:10 then join the 10k which starts at 4:10 pm and finish under 1:45. ~only 50 people registered.

The marathon starts on the waterfront in front of the Radhussen City Hall. There is a big screen set up over the finish line. The porta-potties are rooms in a portable building with men's and women's, very posh and no line! Such a nice start to a race!

The weather is a bit warmer than expected, seems this September all of Europe is facing a warm spell. The half marathoners will suffer more as they run in the warmest part of the day. The marathon course is two laps of the half marathon course. I start at 9:20 am and would love to finish in time to see Gry start her race at 1:30 pm. That goal seems improbable after the Tallinn Marathon, which left me drained and sore.

At 9:20 we are off, heading uphill, running the first two miles of the race through the most expensive residential neighborhood in Norway,

Frogner, very nice! We then turn back towards the center city to run right aside the waterfront marinas with a view looking across the water to Bygdoy, a bit of a peninsula that is also the home of some fabulous museums: They house the Fram polar expedition ship, ancient Viking ships and the Kon-Tiki raft (circa 1947, the balsa raft floated from South America to Polynesia).

We run by the Color Line cruise ship that sails to Kiel, Germany, and then into Aker Brygga, the 80s/90s mixed-use development at the former shipyards right on the waterfront.

From this photo, you can see the office buildings in Aker Brygge across the harbor, the sweeping glass roof of the Astrop Fearnley Museum of Modern Art beyond, and several of the masted schooners along the waterfront.

Bob will be cheering for me as we run back along

the start line at the town hall. He gets a great shot as I run past the Nobel Peace Center. Lots of spectators in this area, -Hee yah, Hee yah, Hee yah is the cheer I hear again and again!

The next mile takes us past the Akershus Castle walls along the waterfront and then up past the Museum of Architecture and through an area of the city that reminds me a bit of Sweden, lovely pristine stone office and apartment buildings and small green spaces.

We quickly turn right and head back out to the waterfront for a breathtaking view of the Norwegian National Opera & Ballet Building. They are staging the War Requiem, -love the graphic and it seems all of Norway loves the building. You can walk  right up to the roof, and it seems to be one of the favorite places to enjoy the sun. There are so many construction cranes along the waterfront! It is bound to look very different for next year's race!

The next section of the race, miles 7 to 8.5 is, hum, -interesting. We continue along the waterfront into an area slated for development. The road surface changes from asphalt to gravel and we are running through a container yard. Not the most scenic, but the change of surface was good for the legs, not great for speed though. This section is an out and back so I see the 3:15, 3:30, 3:45 pace groups as they come by. I am running just behind the 4-hour pace group and feeling good at this point.

I will see Bob again at mile 8.5 in front of the Bar Code buildings, a recent development of modern office buildings that face the waterfront with companies like PWC, DNB, and Deloitte taking up residence. The project

154

was quite controversial, but it seems to add to the life of the renewed waterfront.

Bob catches me as I go up and over the railroad station; it looks a bit crowded, but that's what happens when you run with the pace group.

The next leg of the race takes us through some hills as we climb through the Gronland neighborhood and ultimately around Toyen Park, which is home to the Munch Museum, the Botanical Garden, and the Museum of Natural History. This is a long uphill climb, first the bridge over the train tracks and then a rise of 100' as we run along the park. I stay within sight of the pace group throughout this stretch.

By mile 11.5 we are heading into the very center of the city, on the main pedestrian mall of Karl Johan's Gate, past the Oslo Cathedral, the Parliament Building, and we have cafes lining the course.

I get an unobstructed view of the Royal Palace! I can't believe that we get to run this course and it's kept open all day so the half marathoners get to run the same course. It is spectacular, an authentic tour of the city right down to the brick pavers underfoot!

Then it's back to City Hall Plaza and a 1:58 half for me, a spectacular time after my Tallinn race, and I still feel good. Sweet course so far, I'm happy to be running it twice!

There is no point in my pushing super hard in the second half, it's too early to qualify for Boston and I need to train for Rehoboth in December, that is the race I will target for a fast finish.

I see Bob again at miles 18 and 24. This race was perfect for spectating. Bob selected his cheer spots ahead of time and we marked them on my pace band, even noting which side of the road he would be on. It worked perfectly! He had no trouble getting around the course, taking pictures, and handing me a bit of Gu and ice water.

On the second loop, the views were still spectacular. I used the water stops; volunteers offering water, Maxim drink, and bananas manned them. There was one special stop at mile 17 that offered just coffee and Coke!

~but no GU stops anywhere. My one check in the "con" column. I took a toilet break along the way. No one at the porta-potties! - Amazing!

I was tuckered out when Bob took this shot, 800 meters before the finish. To be honest, I was growing impatient for the end. My watch said 26.6 and my legs said "done" but after a little negotiating...

I hit the finish in 4:13, just in time to pick up my medal and watch Gry start on her adventure.

We celebrate with tapas and beer, 2 marathons in six days, stronger in the second race! Marathons leave you battered and tattered, but I felt good Saturday, Sunday, and was ready to run hard

again by Tuesday! I am taking a break anyway. My next adventure is Trailfest in October with three shorter trail races, 13 miles in Bryce Canyon on day 1, 12 miles at Zion on day 2, and then 18 miles on the north rim of the Grand Canyon on day 3. I am going with some of my favorite runners! Then I run the NY City Marathon (marathon #50) in November and I will finish the year with a fast run at the Rehoboth Beach Marathon in December, adding the state of Delaware to my 50+1 state list.

Chapter 23: Kigali International Peace Marathon

Date: May 21, 2017, start 7:30 am half marathon, 7:45 am for the marathon & 7K, Kigali, Rwanda

Weather: Sunny, 68F at start, high of 75F

Starting elevation: 4,711 feet, Total ascent: 1660 feet

Promoting peace after the 1994 Genocide against the Tutsi that claimed over one million lives in 100 days....

The Kigali International Peace Marathon is run to reinforce the spirit of community, reconciliation, and peace in Rwanda. In that spirit, we spent our Saturday before the race at the Genocide Museum in Kigali, three very intense hours as we were educated on the history of the relations between the Belgians, Hutu, and Tutsi people, the numerous acts of war and genocide that took place before 1994 and finally the infamous genocide of 1994.

After the marathon, we went out to the Nyamata Church Genocide Museum, where some of the worst killings took place. Families that sought sanctuary in the church were executed along with villagers in the surrounding area, over 10,000 were killed and the church has become a place of remembrance. The local villagers have brought the human remains to the church. The pews display mounds of blood-stained clothing of the dead, human remains are in the basement and tombs around the church. Shrapnel holes are still in the walls and ceiling. Our guide was frank and honest in her discussion of the events of 1994.

Nyamata was one of the darkest, most difficult things I have ever experienced. One cannot leave these genocide museums and feel good about humanity. Through our travels around Rwanda, we did feel good about the leadership and resilience of the Rwandan people. Keep reading and you will understand why. I have included two photos, not my own, which better convey the visual experience of Nyamata:

On the morning of the race, we met Julie and her husband Cabo, a couple working in Burundi that came to Kigali to run the half marathon. Julie is from the US and works at the Village Health Center in Burundi, Cabo is from The Gambia. Over the next day, we learned about the work they do in a very remote area of the poorest country in the world, Burundi.

We rode over to the start at Amahoro Soccer Stadium with Julie and Cabo, got as close as we could, and walked to the stadium. Security was tight as it has been all over in Kigali, so we each went through a bag check and a pat-down. Julie and Cabo had to register, so Bob and I said

goodbye and went to look for bag check. It did not exist, but the race staff kindly took our bag along with that of a few elite runners and stored them for us. This is a photo of Bob, Julie, and Cabo as they line up for the start of the half marathon.

Notice all the yellow shirts at the race start? We, runners, were given our "kit" at bib pick-up and here we are expected to wear the shirt during the race. Bob and I could only get size XL since they ran out of smaller sizes so no official "kit" for the race, bummer!

I saw an Australian runner with a Bagan Temple Myanmar Marathon shirt so struck up a conversation. We decided to start the marathon together and ran the first 5K together until I saw Bob on the course and had to stop to capture him running uphill.

A little about the course, the half marathon is a single loop, marathoners do a double loop. The start is inside the Amahoro soccer stadium. After a lap around the outside of the stadium we head out to the Kisementi roundabout, a busy local shopping area, then past the Ministry of Natural Resources, the Rwanda Development Board and then begin the first out and back segment through a mixed residential area with numerous restaurants and small shops. Runners climb most of this section until arriving at the peak by the Aberdeen House (mile 4). We then coast downhill and return from whence we came, uphill again. As we see the Rwanda Development Board, we turn right for the second out and back segment heading past the Rwandan Parliament, the new convention center, and Ninzi Hill before turning around to head back to the stadium.

Funny enough, the Rwandans do not cheer, it is the ex-pats that cheer for us. What we hear is singing, there are lots of churches in the area and we hear the singing as we run by. The thought of it still brings a smile to my face!

This photo is taken as we run up to Aberdeen House the steepest of the hill climbs in the race, ~are you starting to see a theme in the photos?

Rwanda, Land of 1,000 Hills; the Kigali Peace Marathon showed us that it is more than just a slogan! As we crested the hill, we went around it and then started back towards the stadium. Eventually, we got to see the runners behind us, but I never caught sight of Bob.

Bad news at mile 6, the water station had no more water. I still had my water so was not too concerned, but that was not the case for many others, and it was starting to get warm. Most of the 2,000+ runners were men, most runners did the half marathon and the 7K run, perhaps 150 did the marathon. The field was primarily African, but I saw and met several Europeans and Americans. The Africans were fast but also slow, some raced and others just wanted to finish. There was also another Marathon Maniac/Globetrotter there, but unfortunately, we did not meet each other.

As we got closer to the stadium, we started another climb past the Parliament Building, which sits above the wall to the left in the photo. The streets along the course were quite lovely, and I loved the black and white striped curbs, great for safety and it seems to unify the city aesthetically.

The next major site is the new convention center. Its roof resembles a native hut, and at night it is lit up in changing colors. It has become a highlight of the evening skyline since you can see it across the hills of the city.

Mile 9 and still no water so I ask the volunteers if they will have more for us as we make the second loop, "sorry no more water." I still have water but a bit of panic starts to set in, no more water, hot sun, no money for bottled water, and the city water is unsafe to drink. I feel like I have to do the second lap, but wonder if it is sheer stupidity to attempt it??

We circle the stadium before splitting off. The half marathoners run into the stadium for their moment of glory at the finish line. The marathoners head out for another loop. I thought long and hard about going out again. The lack of water made me nervous, but my legs kept moving while my mind was debating, and I pass the split. My reward was a volunteer handing me a full bottle of water before I left the stadium grounds…YAH!

The second loop was not as difficult as I thought it would be. I passed lots of walkers and I followed a program of walking the steep sections and running the downhill. There were fewer runners out, but I always had someone in my sight. I saw my Australian "buddy" who was still looking strong at mile 17. I always had water but never saw a porta-potty so I am not sure what toilets were meant for us along the way. The course had loads of security, there were uniformed officers with rifles at all major buildings and points along the course. I felt like I had access to help if I needed it.

As I approached mile 21, I started to see cars on the course and it soon became apparent that the course was now open to traffic. In the meantime, Bob was waiting for the ceremony at the stadium, and promptly at noon the prizes for the top finishers in the half and full marathon were awarded. A Rwandan woman took first in the half marathon bringing joyful pride to the locals because Kenyans typically sweep the prize money, ~no Rwandan has ever won an event. The first prize was 1.4 million Rwandan francs, roughly equivalent to $10,000, a significant sum in the Rwandan economy. After the awards, the Rwandan President gave a speech followed by a speech from his wife who was the government athletics sponsor. As soon as she finished all the tents and banners were taken down and the stadium cleared out.

Meanwhile, out on the course I arrived at the Kisementi roundabout right after the ceremony. The streets were packed with half marathon finishers, shoppers, pedestrians, motorbikes, and cars. I saw an African runner ahead of me and followed him as we weaved through the crowds and then onward to the stadium. We never saw any marshals, the water stations were taken down but thank goodness, the timing clock inside the stadium was up. Here is a photo of me crossing the finish, third to the last female!

Sadly, the race director had run out of medals and water, plus there was no food available. Bob was there to offer abundant cheer and moral support. We hung out to cheer other marathon finishers. We met another terrific young marathoner from

Burundi and a woman who was waiting for her marathoning husband whom we learned was from Pelham, NY (but they were now living in Kigali)! Our taxicab driver from the previous day showed up inside the stadium and gave us a lift back to the hotel. Another stroke of good fortune.

So, did I enjoy it? -yes, but this was a tough race. In retrospect, things seemed to fall miraculously into place for me! The lack of water caused lots of problems, and the lack of medals for the marathoners caused varying degrees of anger (and violence) among the participants. For me, it was not really about racing; it was the experience of running a marathon in Africa. I met amazing people. I became quite familiar with the city of Kigali, and this race gave me the courage to try another race in African.

When we travel to these races, it is usually an excuse to sightsee and learn about the culture. After the marathon, we took a trip to Akagera Game

Park on the border of Tanzania and Rwanda. As we entered the park, we saw a leopard, a rare sight, and a great opener to the next day's safari drive. We learned about the Grey Crowned Crane Project; Akagera repatriated cranes back to the park, with much success.

After a day at Akagera, we went to the western border of Rwanda, near Uganda and Congo to Volcano National Park to see the Mountain Gorillas, to hike up the volcano to Dian Fossey's research camp, and to see the rare golden monkeys.

I had intimate moments hiking with our guide and guards to the Karisoke Research Center founded by Dian Fossey. Our young  guard talked about his experience as a peacekeeper with the military. He felt a responsibility to be in other areas of Africa where genocide was occurring so he could be part of the solution. He could explain from the heart the effect the atrocities have on society and its people. We came away from Rwanda with so many memories but that conversation is the memory that has stayed with me the longest. I left with hope!

Chapter 24: Race to The Tower

Date: June 10/11, 2017; 53 miles, two marathons in two days event, starts in Stroud, UK

Weather: Windy both days, overcast Saturday, Sunny Sunday

Participants: 800 in total, 329 through racers, and 269 overnight racers finished

Day 1: 27.21 miles, 4,132' climb, 6:04:42 finish

Day 2: 27.36 miles, 3,658' climb, 6:03:45 finish

Conquer the Cotswold Way.....

Race to the Tower is run on a section of the 102-mile Cotswold Way, a UK National Trail. We started just outside the town of Stroud and finished at Broadway Tower. I did the course as a two-day event, so ran two marathons in two days. Why? Because next year I plan to run Comrades Ultra Marathon in South Africa, the pinnacle of running in Africa, so I need a tough race this summer to test my stamina.

The race started in a field at the Bird in Hand Farm. We had a big tent to keep us out of the wind. Heineken, the race sponsor, had a team of over 250 people, mostly super friendly walkers, full of spirit. The 800

participants went out in four waves, 8:00, 8:15, 8:30, and 8:45... I was off with the 8:15 group.

I saw Bob, the lone spectator, in Painswick, a lovely village we run through early in the race.

Then he is off to start his garden tours and meet up with Jess and Josie. I ran at a nice easy trail pace as we went through the woodlands and fields, my speed in check because there are so many runners on the trail.

Next is the 700' climb to Painswick Beacon at mile 7 and a series of rolling hills through beech woodlands which takes me up Coopers Hill, the site of the crazy cheese rolling competition you may have heard about. At that race competitors follow a nine-pound wheel of cheese down a hill, racing each other to the bottom. See photo (not mine) of the hill they run.

Our big descent comes at mile 14, and then we hit the second aid station. The volunteers offer us so many fueling options, 4 different quinoa bars, High5 gel, candy bars, bananas, nuts, chips, squash (a fruit drink in the UK), flat coke, and rehydration drink. Each fueling station is slightly different, but all are equally enticing, so you have to force yourself to quickly make selections and move on.

In my enthusiasm I left the aid station and tried to pick up the pace, I missed a sign and ran about a half-mile off course down a beautiful flat trail with a black dog on my heels. I lost the dog then realized there was no one else on the trail, Ughh! I had to run back past the dog. He was on my heels again until the owner finally called him off.

Back on course, I am rewarded with another 600' hill climb to Crickley Hill at mile 18, which has a beautiful

overlook to the valley below. These big hill climbs give me a chance to walk but my heart is beating so hard that it is only a break for the legs, not the lungs! Lots of ups and downs take us to the famous Devils Chimney rock formation and Leckhampton Hill....at this point I was tired so I missed the Devils Chimney??

The trails have been muddy in the woodlands because of last week's rain. I have worn a newish pair of trail shoes and they have served me well, no blisters. The medical kit we were advised to carry has six band-aids...won't be needing those...along with sun cream.... won't be needing that either.... tick spray, alcohol hand wipes for sanitizing scrapes, lots of paracetamol, Pepto Bismol pills, stretchable tape, Vaseline and a bit of spare food. I feel slightly over-prepared but had I fallen somewhere all this would have been quite handy!

The last six miles hold another climb and take us to Aggs Farm, our base camp... which is heaven.

Food....yes Italian, Mexican and best of all the "Ministry of Cake" is here!

Race to the Tower Tent City

Hot portable showers, hot portable sinks, and who can trail race without a pamper station?

Day 2 is a much more casual start, leave when you are ready! At mile 3 we climbed up to the highest point of the entire two-day race, Cleeve Hill, glad to hit it early in the day. The next highlight was Bels Knap Long Barrow, a 5,000-year-old mounded burial chamber for 38 people.

In my enthusiasm, I strayed off the course yet again, but only a few hundred yards this time. Off to Winchcombe, I go, past the ruins of the Cistercian monastery called Hailes Abbey, a few miles outside of Winchcombe.

169

By mile 15 we are in the lovely little village of Stanway after having made yet another big hill climb. This is Stanway House.

Then into the village of Buckland at mile 21, a Broadway finish is on my mind! I am so ready to be done. I enter Broadway village looking for the finish but learn that we run through the village and then ascend the last hill, an 800' climb from the village up to Broadway Tower, such wickedness. I did try to run the hill, but it was ridiculously steep!

Here I am crossing the finish line, so happy! 6:03:45, a better time than yesterday.....

Chapter 25: Petrified Forest Marathon

Date: October 21, 2017, 7:15am, Arizona, USA

Weather: morning low of 39F degrees, high of 59F

Participants: 40 runners

It is still forest here, the forest of used-to-be.

Its trees are the trees of memory.

> Their branches — so many tongues, so many hands —

> They still speak a story to those who will listen.

By only looking without listening, you will not hear the trees.

You will see only hard stone and flattened landscape,

> But if you're quiet, you will hear it.

> Faithful Forest ~by Alberto Ríos

Do you remember the *Highlights* magazine? Back in the early '70s, I was smitten with Arizona's Petrified Forest because of an article in that magazine. Trees that turned to stone before dinosaurs walked the earth, astounding! It stuck with me for almost 50 years. Second, I love our National Parks. They exist because we the people agreed they housed something truly unique, something so special that all people should witness and experience it at

minimal expense. If I can be lucky enough to run a marathon and experience a national park, sign me up!

Our adventure started with a family wedding, perfectly timed so I could consider this race. Bob's clan gathered in the desert at the base of the Superstition Mountains just east of Phoenix with the saguaro cactus, red mountains, and ghost towns, gorgeous!

Stage 2 took the four of us, Jess, Josie, Bob, and I, to Sedona for four full days of red canyon sightseeing and the best trail running I have ever done! Add to that yoga, spas, more than a few vortexes, Flagstaff skiing, and Phoenix airport, this may be the new post-NYC home for Bob & Cheryl, ~until we visit in the heat of summer.

We discovered this unique Peace Park in Sedona, which features a Buddhist temple and a statue of Buddha. The Sedona Amitabha Stupa is a sacred place, but you don't have to be a Buddhist to visit, all are welcome including an inquisitive three-year-old!

Here is a picture of one of the Sedona trails. There are enough trails to run a new one every day for a month.

Stage 3 brought us two hours east of Flagstaff, along the way we stopped to see ancient Indian cliff dwellings at Walnut Canyon and the Meteor Crater, both very worthy side trips. A fun fact about the Meteor Crater; the crater would house 20 NFL football fields and stadium seating for 2 million people. Imagine that football fans!

We stayed in the city of Holbrooke, on Route 66, a town known for being "too rough for women and churches." ~Our destination was the Wigwam Motel, a 1950s historic landmark...

Stage 4, the race... The Wigwam Motel served as race headquarters for the bib pick-up, pre-race pasta dinner, and post-race BBQ. At the pre-race pasta dinner, we met a first-time marathoner who spent two years losing almost 200 pounds so he could run this race. His best advice was to find a goal that is so important to you that your weight loss becomes a key part of your life plan. Excess food is your enemy, sabotaging your goal. His quest and his advice seemed truly inspired. Who would have thought this challenging little race would be so meaningful?

A little on the race logistics: The Petrified Forest has two entrances, the North entrance looks out over the Painted Desert, then down the park road, 28 miles south you find the South entrance and the Rainbow Forest Museum. A road just itching to host marathon runners! Temperatures in

Phoenix hit 98 degrees but up here at elevation 5500' we start the race at 44 degrees and finished at 66 degrees. The wind can be a factor. The day before we stood at the Meteor Crater and the gusts were 40 mph, but luckily it passed through and we had a light breeze on race day.

I had to catch the race bus at 6 am at the South park entrance. On the drive, through the park, I talked with another first-time marathoner, a triathlete Packer fan from Milwaukee that had just moved to Phoenix. Along the way, we got a sense of the course (hilly) and saw both a herd of pronghorn and another of mule deer sporting some gorgeous fall antlers.

After a short wait at the race start, we were off…the first two miles were

uphill at an elevation of 5700' but, what took your breath away was the scenery! The Painted Desert at 7:20 am is a layering of colored hills, red, yellow, brown, and green that stretches for over one hundred miles. ~Spectacular! Let's see what else we can discover!

174

After the Painted Desert, we run a slight downhill for miles through the immense grasslands at the northern end of the park.

The course starts to rise uphill, and the scenery changes through the Blue Mesa and Tepees at the mid-point of the race. We see scattered petrified wood; the terrain is surreal. As the softer soil erodes, 200 million-year-old petrified logs are revealed as they were left in the Triassic Age.

This photo is taken at mile 18, as we climb the big hill past Agate Bridge to the Jasper Forest. The next 5 miles are a gentle climb to get over the Flat Tops. The final two miles are a downhill dash to the Rainbow Forest Museum. I can see for miles and miles!

I came in 3rd woman overall in a small field of runners (69 starters). My trophy is a big chunk of petrified wood which seems so appropriate given my lifelong curiosity for the park and its petrified trees. The medal is a Kokopelli statue mounted on locally harvested limestone, very nice! The finish line has a "Harvey Girl" and the Holbrook High School Choir as volunteers, a massage tent, water, and snacks. We had free access to the park for the day, which we took full advantage of.

That evening we sat around a campfire at the post-race BBQ with the race director, her team, some choir kids, and a few runners reminiscing about the race highlights. We learned about the history of Holbrook and developed a true appreciation for the local people hosting the race. What an opportunity the Petrified Forest National Park and the City of Holbrook have provided for us, such a memorable marathon event!

Chapter 26: Firenze Marathon

Date: November 26, 2017, 8:30 am, Florence, Italy

Weather: High 50F and then cooled to 43F, rainy

Participants: 10,000 registrants, 8,600 finishers

Blue Bag of Happiness Brings out the Sunshine in Me.........

This was my third trip to Florence. On my first trip, I was an architectural student backpacking the "grand parade of Europe" during my summer of learning in 1981. My second was a quick day trip while I was in Italy buying stone for a lobby on Park Avenue in the '90s. Bob, who is 99% Italian, was the mastermind behind this trip. He booked a hotel room that looked right out onto the marathon finish and was a block away from my start corral. Awesome place!

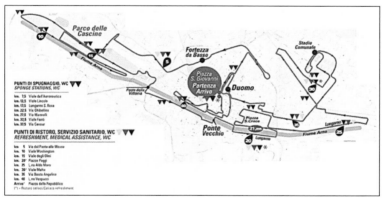

For the runners, the Firenze marathon offers a kid's fun run, but no half marathon or 10K. This is the second-largest race in Italy, with 10,000 runners registered this year. The race starts in the Duomo Plaza, the square which houses the famous Florence Cathedral topped by Brunelleschi's stunning dome, the Baptistery with its famous bronze doors by Ghiberti, and the Campanile or bell tower. We will run through the Duomo Plaza four times during the race, which must have driven tourists crazy, but it was incredible for the runners! The expo is about a half an hour's walk from our hotel to the Campo di Marti athletics complex. There was a good assortment of vendors to peruse, but the highlight is getting the bib and the Italian-designed race t-shirt. The shirt goes to the new runner in the family, our grandson Jude!

A little background before discussing the race. My knee was bothering me. I was limping around the week before the race. I had serious concerns about whether I could get through the course if I had to walk. I used the foam roller all week long to loosen the muscles around the knee and ran very little and very lightly. By the time we got to Florence, it was feeling much better, but I arrived with a sore throat! I started taking an over-the-counter medication, which is not available in the US called First Defense. It is a spray coating that blocks the cold virus from permeating the membranes of the nose. The cold did not move past the sore throat phase so I went into the race slightly ill but with no fever and no congestion in my chest. I was not sure how it would go for me out there????

Now the weather.... every time I checked, the weather in Florence was sunny with temperatures between 52-57 degrees. I did not pack my waterproof coat but brought a plastic bag just in case of rain. On Friday, two days before the race, the weather forecast took a turn, rain in the early morning, clearing off by 9:00. The forecast got worse as time went on. Luckily, the pre-race goody bag included a thick plastic blue poncho for us to wear to stay warm and dry at the race start. Those blue bags were my godsend, Cheryl + cold + rain = misery!

OK, enough negativity, it was a great race, but it seems important to let you know where my typically upbeat and positive head was days before the race!

We did some great carb-loading on Saturday, lunch was a huge calzone and dinner was a delicious bowl of Pappa al Pomodoro, tomato, and bread soup! Typically, I would eat the traditional marathoner's spaghetti, but this seemed so much more adventurous.

Race day we opened the shutters and see dark skies, but no rain. I check the weather which says rain at 9 am and by noon it should start to clear off, temps will get

colder as the day goes on and the wind gets stronger. I dress in tights and lots of throw-away layers. Bob and I leave the hotel at 7:50 with a race start at 8:30, sweet! We had no trouble getting to my corral in the Plaza di Republic and at 8 am he leaves me to go watch the start.

Above is a photo of the start, unreal to think that this plaza and this city which I learned so much about in architecture school hosts a marathon. I feel quite fortunate to be here.

I dropped my throw-away clothes and blue bag as we got started and after a kilometer of running the light rain started! I scoured the sidewalks looking for a discarded blue bag and as luck would have it someone dropped an unopened blue bag, -my deliverance! I was surprised that more folks did not use the same trick, I guess my experience suffering in the rain at the Hartford Marathon was a great lesson learned.

At 6k we enter the largest park in Florence, the Cascine, on the right bank of the Arno River. We are in the park for 10k and get to see the lead runners on the out and back. They ran right next to me. Gosh, their speed and fast leg turnover left quite an impression!

179

While we run in the park it is pouring rain, most of my fellow runners are drenched and a few of the elites have already dropped out.

Here is a photo as we leave the park and run alongside the Arno River back towards the historic city center.

We will run across the famous Ponte Vecchio Bridge which I find inexplicable. The tiny bridge is always dense-packed with tourists, both sides of it are lined with little jewelry shops. It's the major tourist route to get between the left and right banks of

the Arno River. How is this going to work? We easily run over the bridge while listening to the cheers of the crowd. ~Such a thrill.

We are running through the historic city center towards the Basilica di Santa Croce and its plaza. I expect to see Bob by the plaza, but no luck.

The wet weather took another turn for the worse, the temperatures dropped and the wind picked up. I was happy to be modeling this season's fashionable blue bag!

We continue back to run along the Arno River and make our way through residential neighborhoods to the Asics Firenze Marathon Stadium "Luigi Ridolfi" and take ¾ of a lap around the track. As we leave the stadium, we

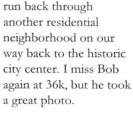

run back through another residential neighborhood on our way back to the historic city center. I miss Bob again at 36k, but he took a great photo.

We pass through the Duomo Plaza again, past the Academy, home of Michelangelo's David, through Piazza San Marco, and then past the famous Medici Palace and through the Duomo Plaza again. The course is spectacular and we are seeing the city's best sights. Then it is past The Bargello, home of Donatello's David, past Palazzo Vecchio, and right through the courtyard of the Uffizi Gallery!

It is super exciting to run through these gorgeous streets, past prominent city treasures, plus the sun is finally coming out. My pace has quickened the last few miles and I am ready to ditch my beloved blue bag! The last 3k takes us along the Arno and back through the historic city center to finish at the Duomo Plaza.

Twenty-five countries are complete, that

is cause for celebration! A big thank you to Kathy for suggesting this race! I was thinking Rome was my Italian race, but Florence was always my favorite city in Italy and this race was fantastic. I loved the course. It is flat and you see so many incredible sights. The local streets are picture-perfect; you have easy to access affordable hotels next to the start/finish line, enthusiastic volunteers, and spectators... even in the rain. The race has an extensive field of runners but spacious streets meant it never felt crowded.

If the scenery and history haven't won you over, then perhaps the food; our post-race glass of Chianti served with a spicy mini cheese sandwich and olives.... or our celebration meal at a local trattoria with fresh artichoke salad, amazing aged Florentine beef, garlic spinach, and more Chianti! -or Monday's lunch of shaved salami and pecorino cheeses and yes, a bit of gelato, Ciao Bella!! (Hello Beautiful).

PART IV: The Ultra Marathoner-More Than 26.2

In 2012, I was at the expo for my very first marathon in Philadelphia. All the vendors selling runners gear, race nutrition, post-race balms, and therapies overwhelmed me, and then a young man approached me, suggesting I run the Comrades Marathon. He told me it was the best race in Africa, and Africa had the best runners in the world. He was a genuine salesman with a great hook. Then he told me it was 90 kilometers, I laughed at him. I was worried about running 42 kilometers in Philadelphia! My goal in 2012 was one marathon, check that off the life list and move on. We chatted for some time and he continued to sing the praises of the race. I took the brochure, and it made it home to find a spot next to my computer. Running that race gnawed at me over the years. It became a marker for my acceptance of myself as a serious runner.

My next race report discusses my 2018 Comrades race experience in detail. It does not discuss the health challenges I faced in the summer of 2018. I spent the winter working on the toughest training plan I had ever developed for myself in preparation for Comrades. I had a random physical in mid-May and the doctor found a lump under my left arm. A mammogram and a biopsy were done that week. I had DCIS, an early stage of breast cancer. I would need to have the cancerous tissue removed and follow that with radiation treatments.

I quickly made an appointment for breast surgery before I left New York at the end of May for London and South Africa. I spent three weeks in South Africa traveling and running the Comrades Marathon. I returned to New York in mid-June for the surgery. Once I had the doctor's approval, I returned to the UK and continued training for the 50K Black RAT race which was in early August. Bob and I returned to New York immediately after the RAT race so I could start my radiation treatments. I continued my training throughout the treatments, running in the morning, radiation treatments in the early afternoon, completing my treatments after Labor Day. The day the treatments finished, we traveled to Wisconsin to visit my mother in her new independent living apartment; then took a road trip to Iowa to run another ultra.

You might wonder why?

I signed up for the races before I was diagnosed with cancer and before my Mom sold the childhood home to move into independent living. I had a deep need to stay normal and minimize the impact of the cancer treatment, ~just carry on. In retrospect, I believe that my continued training and fitness helped me handle and recover from the surgery and radiation better than most patients.

At the time, I could not conceive of taking a DNS (did not start) for my races. I liked that my focus was on my running and that I was succeeding at these tough races. I felt normal. I kept a positive attitude through my cancer treatments knowing that it was a process with a start and finish. The elation and sense of personal pride that I felt crossing each finish line that summer was worth the small hurdles I faced training during my treatment.

The Black RAT (Roseland August Trail) Race, is a 32-mile trail race on the stunning South Cornwall Coastal Path on the English Channel. The race offered spectacular "coastal scenery, over undulating paths, through fields, villages, and surrounding countryside – it is not for the faint-hearted!" I had kayaked this section of the coast before but had not done the Coastal Path. The race was stunning! The total elevation climb was 6,800' and not a race for those with a fear of heights! I came back again in 2019 and signed up for 2020 hoping (unsuccessfully!) to make that race my 100th marathon, more on that in Chapter 35.

In 2019, I ran on the opposite side of the Cornish coast for the Clovelly Marathon. It is run on the North Devon and Cornwall Coastal Path between Clovelly and Bude, a gorgeous and rugged stretch of the Atlantic coast. The coast is known for its ascents and descents, my ascent total was 5,800'.

I continued to run road marathons, scheduling in my favorites from the marathon majors; London, Boston, and New York City. I continued to work on running a marathon in each of the fifty-states adding ten more states for a total of 38 states completed. I ran a new personal record for speed at the Revel Big Bear Marathon, posting a time of 3:40;49 in 2018 and then in 2019 I ran again finishing with 3:40:21. It was a highly productive and rewarding time for me until March of 2020 and the onset of the coronavirus pandemic. Racing went on pause along with so many other things.

This ultra-marathoner ran twenty-eight races in twenty-eight months. Ten of the races were ultra-marathons. I wrote eleven race reports which are highlighted in grey. The eleven are a very diverse scenic set of races:

	RACE	Date	Location	Time
73	Comrades Ultramarathon	10-Jun-18	Durban, ZAF	11:11:26
74	Roseland August Trail-50K	10-Aug-18	Porthpean, GBR	7:20:45
75	Pleasant Creek Trail-45K	15-Sep-18	Palo, IA	6:01:14
76	Revel Big Bear	14-Oct-18	Redlands, CA	3:40:49
77	New York City Marathon	4-Nov-18	New York, NY	4:18:00
78	Valencia Marathon	2-Dec-18	Valencia, SPN	4:06:27
79	Louisiana Marathon	19-Jan-19	Baton Rouge, LA	4:09:34
80	Big Beach Marathon	27-Jan-19	Gulf Shores, AL	4:12:37
81	Mississippi Blues Marathon	28-Jan-19	Jackson, MS	4:12:13
82	Post Oak Challenge	22-Feb-19	Tulsa, OK	5:53:01
83	Antelope Canyon-50M	9-Mar-19	Page, AZ	12:18:33
84	Boston Marathon	15-Apr-19	Boston, MA	4:15:30
85	Belfast Marathon	5-May-19	Belfast, NI	3:58:36
86	Thunder Dragon Marathon	26-May-19	Paro, BHTN	5:48:25
87	Clovelly Marathon	22-Jun-19	Clovelly, GB	6:33:21
88	Race to the Stones-50K	13-Jul-19	Lewknor, GBR	6:14:01
89	Race to the Stones-50K	14-Jul-19	Wantage, GBR	6:04:22
90	Roseland August Trail-50K	10-Aug-19	Porthpean, GBR	7:39:43
91	Green River Marathon	1-Sep-19	Marlborough, VT	3:47:31
92	Cheyenne Marathon	15-Sep-19	Cheyenne, WY	4:22:35
93	Fallfest	21-Sep-19	Westminster, CO	4:50:25

	RACE	Date	Location	Time
94	New York City Marathon	3-Nov-19	New York, NY	4:21:46
95	Revel Big Bear	9-Nov-19	Redlands, CA	3:40:21
96	Arches Ultra-50K	25-Jan-20	Moab, UT	5:55:56
97	Atlanta Marathon	1-Mar-20	Atlanta, GA	4:28:22
98	The Round Reading Ultra	1-Aug-20	Reading, GBR	5:52:15
99	2020 Plym Trail Marathon	12-Sep-20	Clearbrook, GBR	4:29:46
100	Nearly But Not Quite London Marathon	4-Oct-20	Staines-upon-Thames, GBR	4:48:45

Chapter 27: Comrades Marathon

Date: June 10, 2018; 5:30 am, Durban, South Africa

Pietermaritzburg to Durban, 90.184 k/56 miles

Weather: high 74F, overcast skies

Finish Time: 11:11:26 (12-minute pace), 231 out of 608 in age group W50-59

Garmin: Elevation Gain 3,642', Elevation Loss 5,794'

ASIJIKI - NO TURNING BACK.....

Comrades Marathon "South Africa's Super Bowl" is a revered institution in South Africa. You must finish the 90k race in under 12 hours, the ultimate human race. They cover the full twelve hours on television with highlights of the race, interviews with the winners, and loads of coverage of everyday runners like me. Here is some background: Comrades is a point-to-point race with the even years going downhill and the odd years going uphill. Downhill is a misnomer... I still ran an elevation gain of 3,642' and the down race is 2k longer than the uphill route! In my heart, I still believe it has got to be the easier version of the two options? We start in Pietermaritzburg, the capital of Kwa Zululand, with a population of about 250,000. We finish in Durban, a population of 3.5 million and a city famed for its beaches, port, and Indian population.

Why this race? In 2012, a Comrades ambassador suggested that I sign up, and I quickly told him I could never run 56 miles! It is amazing how ideas get planted in your head and it gnawed at me (Africa+Running=Safari). The more I learned, the more I felt like it could be the penultimate challenge to my running career!

I trained hard all winter and ran 50-60 miles per week during February, March, and April. I could feel the increased distance taking a toll on my body, but thanks to massage and physical therapies I went into the race feeling great! I was lucky enough to have a training partner all winter long (Thank-you Tracie!) and she joined me for a good portion of the race.

Tracie and I took a six-hour bus trip along the course two days before the race. It was fantastic to be more familiar with the course, but daunting too. If anyone else considers the race, I would suggest taking the trip, the familiarity with the course far outweighs the trepidation you feel on tour...

We stayed in a hotel in Durban along the Golden Mile on the beach. For Durban based runners there is an option to take a 3:00 am bus to the 5:30 am race start 56 miles away in Pietermaritzburg. That meant a 1:45 am wake-up call to be ready for the 2:30 am cab, which is not a great way to start the day! Here we are, cold but smiling and ready to roll out into the darkness! ASIJIKI - No Turning Back, this year's official motto for the race!! Here is the elevation chart:

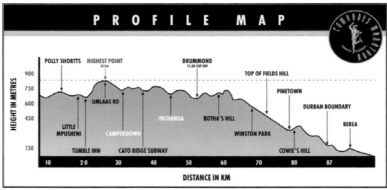

As we run, we will be looking for Bob and Tracie's children, Jake and Katelyn, who are spectating at 21k/13.1 miles. They caught a 4 am bus and will be enjoying a champagne brunch along the sidelines while waiting for us to make an appearance. Before we see them, we must climb many hills. The first, Polly Shorts, we climb in the pitch-black darkness, and the second, Little Polly's, we climb just as the sun rises.

After greeting the sunlight, we carry on past the first cut-off at Lion Park (cut off is 2.5 hours, no problem!) to meet up with the family and pick up

our first package of supplies for the next stage of the race. I am trying a nutrition strategy suggested by Coach Mike from my Hyland's Team. I run well with Hammer and Gu so was advised to increase my intake but dilute my gels with water. I premixed 6 packs of Hammer gel with 1.5 cups of water, which Bob handed to me at mile 13 in a water bottle. I loved the taste treat and it was very effective fueling!

Next was Umlass Road, a 4k climb to 810 meters, the highest point of the race. Up here in the "Land of 10,000 Hills", the views are fantastic!

I will not see Bob again until 69k where he will be enjoying a braai or a South African barbecue with all his fellow spectators. In the meantime, there are still loads of hills to climb along the way. The course is quite crowded but the views are lovely. I think we make an impressive sight for the South African spectators that are out to see us. Lots of families are out collecting all the tossed shirts, gloves, and blankets we no longer need to keep us warm.

At 33k we see the Ethembeni School which we visited a few days earlier. The kids were out along the school giving us high fives! The school is home to about 300 kids from KwaZululand that suffer from disabilities including albinism. Albinos are still abducted in parts of Africa and murdered for body parts, ~yes, true! I was shocked but it happens in Tanzania, Burundi, and even South Africa. The kids at this school are in a place where their unique talents are allowed to shine. It was a treat to spend time with them and hear their cheers along the route!

By mile 20 Tracie is starting to suffer immensely from jet lag and lack of sleep. We stay together until we are passed by the 11:30 "bus" at roughly 26 miles which requires an explanation. A "bus" is a big group of people that are running with a pacer, it can be an official pacer or an unofficial one. The race has a 12-hour cut off so we needed to stay ahead of this 11:30 group.

I ran alongside the 11:30 "bus" for quite some time. There was a "bus driver" who decides when people should walk with a countdown 1, 2, 3... walk. and then when it was time to run the reverse... 3, 2, 1 run. The group had at least 70 runners, so I either joined or had to run ahead. I went just ahead and used them to gauge my progress up the hills and as a source of entertainment. I had no headphones, so the singing and antics

were entertaining! All I can say is, there are many hills until you get to 60k. We climbed Drummond Hill, Botha's Hill, and little ones in between, so the bus kept my pace in check. At Drummonds Hill, you are halfway done. There stands the Comrades Wall of Honor, interlocking bricks with

previous runner's names on plaques, and Arthur's Seat, the favorite "resting spot" for Arthur Newton, a 5 times winner of Comrades. Leave a flower in Arthur's seat for a lucky second half. Will my name grace the "Wall"? *(~yes, in 2020 Bob had my name added to the wall!)*

Folks are out with their barbecues cheering us from the sidelines. My team USA shirt was a huge hit and I heard "Go Shee Ril" over and over. I spent a good portion of the race fist-pumping my support back to the spectators. 25% of the runners are female, 1% are from the USA and five of us were named Cheryl, I stood out from the masses.

Water was given in a plastic tube which you had to bite into to get water. It took some finesse, but I liked the system. Later in the race, they also had salted potatoes, oranges, bananas, and flat soda at the water stations. They even had leg massage stations! The spectators were giving out any and everything from candy to beer to bits of BBQ. I stuck to my gels until very late in the race when the flat coke started looking very good! Below is a photo of one of the 42 water stations.

Once we pass 60k it is such a relief because the downhill portion of the

race starts, yah! I look forward to seeing Bob and checking in with him. I am feeling good, with no real aches or pains, and I realize that I will finish the race. At the time, I wanted to get in under 11 hours and that required a huge push downhill, tally ho! ~looking perky at 42 miles with only 16 more miles to go!

I am starting to pass loads of runners now and I keep up the push, "boom chugga lugga, boom chugga lugga." I have an app installed on my watch, which is helping me to forecast my finish time. My pace has been inconsistent because of all the uphill's but now I can start to better use it to forecast my finish; 11 hours could be in my grasp, but it is too early to predict.

We start to hit the outskirts of the city and at 81k I pass the 11 hours cut-off point in 10 hours! ~Now the race starts feeling very, very long and the stadium still seems very far away. The course is flattening out. I keep running (walking uphill but running everything else) until my watch forecasts my finish at 11:02. I know the watch is shorting my distance so I will not make my goal of a sub 11. I am bummed. I start to walk, which was a mistake because I immediately start to feel nauseous. I lost my mojo at 88k, there were very few people around me. I finally got passed by someone and started jogging again. I still had that competitive spirit. We went under an overpass and then I see this beautiful sight, Moses

Mabhida Stadium, built for the 2010 FIFA World Cup and home to my finish line!

As I enter the stadium it is unbelievable! The sun is starting to set and you run through an arch,

into the glowing stadium which seats about 60,000 people. It seems that half the seats are full, 30,000 people are cheering, the commentator is calling off the names of finishers and it feels just exhilarating to be finished! The international runners are immediately led to a separate post-finish area (our entry fee is 10X more than South African runners) where I saw Bob, Tracie, and her children waiting for me, crazy amazing!

Bob and I stayed to watch the 12-hour cut-off; it was so emotional. The 12-hour "bus" came in with 200 people crossing the finish, then the clock ticks down 10, 9, 8... 3, 2, 1, and the rope goes up! The human barrier goes across. There will be no more finishers. Runners collapse on the track from frustration and exhaustion. They are so close to finishing but there is no buffer at Comrades.

I don't plan to give the uphill route a try but if anyone is planning to do Comrades, I recommend it especially if you add in time for an African safari! Our experience here was epic!

Chapter 28: Valencia Marathon

Date: December 2, 2018, 8:30 am start, Valencia, Spain

Weather: 51F at the start and 64F at the finish, sunny

Stats: 22,000 marathon and 8,500/10k; 14,000 runners are from Spain, the rest international but only 65 runners from the USA; 83% of the runners are men

Valencia — 'The Running City'.....

Why the Valencia Marathon? I wanted to run it as a salute to my Valencia sisters. For years they have patiently listened to my Dutch discoveries, so it was time to see what Valencia, The Running City, offered. We found a gorgeous city filled with delightful surprises!

I am going to start this report with a pivotal moment in the history of Valencia. In 1957, a devastating flood occurred on the River Turia which ran around the city center. Several people were killed and the downtown area was devastated by the extensive flooding. Immediately after, the city government started diverting the river. The river bed is now a 5-mile-long park, finished in 1969, and wraps around the upper half of the center city called the Turia Riverbed Gardens.

At one end of the park sits the Santiago Calatrava designed City of Arts and Sciences, a cultural center with five futuristic-looking buildings, four of them designed by Calatrava. This area is the start and finish of our race! This development sits roughly halfway between the old city center and the seaside marina. Calatrava is the architect of the Milwaukee Museum Addition and the World Trade Center Transportation Hub in New York.

I know the Valencia marathon as a fast and flat course. The half marathon, in late October, holds the world record. The city prides itself on

its running traditions. There are running "courses" or paths all over the city, and more are being added. There was a competition for the city center businesses to add running to their store motif so we saw window decorations, runner's decoration on ceramics, and runner merchandise. The race offered activities on Saturday, a 5k breakfast run, a children's race, a paella party, but we missed all those events while out touring.

We had an apartment in the old city, perfect for touring. It's 1.5 miles from the expo, race start, and finish. We took the free (until 4 pm on race day) local city bus to the race start. We had time to drop my baggage and stop at a hotel to hang out pre-race. Bob could escort me to my corral, so we stayed together until I started jogging to the start line. This is so unusual for a race that starts 30,000 people,

amazing! I had no trouble accessing the corral, some folks waited until the last minute to enter, and yet NO problems, ~nice!

Everyone starts the race crossing the Puente de Monteolivete bridge, but the 10k runners quickly turn off to the left while the marathoners head to the seaside and marina area. This is a photo looking at the runners after they crossed the bridge.

As we head towards the marina, I see my first spectator cheering group, a big group of people dressed as circus performers, crazy! At the marina, 3k into the race, I saw the Pamela sculpture by the artist Manolo Valdes. The artist is originally from Valencia but now lives in NYC. This permanent piece was selected by the people of Valencia after a show of

his work and will now stay at the marina. I did not see much of the sea, but the Valdes hat sculpture sure put a smile on my face!

The marina and seaside are about two miles from the city center and got a big facelift after its selection in 2007 as the home of America's Cup race. From there we went through the Cabanyal, an area that once housed the local fisherman's population. It is filled with small unique two-story houses, many faced with Valencia tile in the Art Deco style.

The next section, out and back in the Valencia University area, was not very exciting until, at 52 minutes and 51 seconds, my watch locked up! I had a bit of a panic since I use my watch to track my race progress. I tried a soft reset with no luck, it was still locked up. I contemplated my problem for the next mile and tried the soft reset again. This time it worked! It started tracking time and distance from 52:51, not too helpful.

This is a photo of the runners at around 14k, lovely local streets, and plenty of other runners to keep me company. At 18k we run past the Mestalla Stadium, home of the Valencia Club de Fútbol a Spanish professional football

club with a huge fan base. We retrace our steps and head back to the marina, and then to the City of Arts and Sciences, along the Turia Gardens, entering the old city by the Serranos Towers, the largest Gothic city gateway in Europe.

In the old city, we run by my favorite building, the National Ceramics Museum at 25K. At 28K we run through the plaza for the Ayuntamiento de Valencia (Valencia Town Hall), It is a central gathering space for tourists and locals alike... The spectators are congregating to cheer for us today!

At 30k I finally see Bob and get a much-needed lift to my spirits.

On the topic of inspiration, I continued to see spectator groups all along the way, and they were terrific. I mentioned the circus

group but we also saw the KISS Army Fan Club with about 40 members, a human pyramid, numerous bands, and drum groups. Best of all, a big group of women in traditional dress lining the course

~Traditional dress requires a longer explanation.

Every year on March 19, Valencia celebrates the Las Fallas Festival to welcome spring; it's something I would like to see on another trip. During the festival, people stroll the streets to the Plaza of the Virgin in their traditional dress. The real highlight to me is the installation of over 700 satirical temporary statues (think elaborate floats like Mardi Gras), some

reaching 50' in height. The artists spend a year working on them and then at the end of the festival they are set alight.

~Book your hotel a year in advance!

Back to the race, usually, I talk a little about how I felt during the run. I was quite concerned about this race for two reasons; I had severe hamstring cramping at NYC Marathon on November 4th and I had injured my back while obsessively using the power sander to finish our stairs in Cornwall. I felt really good running this race and held an 8:50 pace until mile 15 or so. After mile 15, I started to feel the normal calf niggles that lead to cramping so I backed off to a 9:30 pace and took a short break while visiting with Bob. I finally got my mojo back after taking a shot of salt and was able to pick the pace back up, yah!

From the city center, we went out to the Valencia Bioparc (zoo) between 33-34k which I was excited about. Why do you wonder? ~Because the

big cheer we heard all over the course was animal, animal, animal! The zoo was a bit of a non-event. We saw leafy boulevards, which were very nice but I wanted giraffes, elephants or zebra in view! We just saw more runners... doing loads of walking.

We turn to head back towards the old city on Avenue Del Cid, a major thoroughfare. The course has been flat wide boulevards, spacious, and ideal for speed. We are on our way to the Valencia North Train Station and Plaza de Toros de Valencia, the Valencia Bullring. Bullfights are still held in this coliseum all year long. The most important fights are held during the Las Fallas festival in March. At 40K we run by the La Puerta del Mar, Gateway to the Sea, built in 1946 in imitation of the city gate that stood here. This city weaves together the old and the new or recreates the old from the new!

I saw Bob again at 41k. I was feeling good. I had been passing many

runners, but the excitement of the finish line rallied everyone. It was such a thrill running into the skeletal architecture at the City of Arts and Sciences! We run over the pool and finish between the Umbracle and the Science Museum,

looking at the Hemisferic, it feels like I am in a George Jetson space-age cartoon setting! The finish was spectacular!!

The course deserves its reputation for being flat and fast, I finished in 3:58:19.... oops, remember my watch was off for almost a mile... so 4:06:27. I am quite happy with that!

~The Spanish food is excellent! The Valencia oranges are prolific and tasty! The Spaniards make a great drink called agua de Valencia. A mixture of Spanish champagne, gin, vodka, and Valencia orange juice. Combine that with delicious post-race tapas or the unique Valencia style paella...but only one agua de Valencia or you might see stars!

Chapter 29: Antelope Canyon Ultra Marathon

Date: March 9, 2019, 5:45 am start in Page, Arizona, the 50-mile distance

Weather: Low 40's start with high 50's for the day

Finish time: 12:18:34 (pace of 14:45 minute miles), 1st out of 4 finishers in my age group W55-59.

Garmin Stats: 4,163 elevation gain & 4,094 loss, Elevation at Page: 4,000'

Natures Artwork, Oh Does It Delight…..

This race has been on my "must-do" list for years. I waited to sign up because it's 50 miles running with most of the course in the sand, so very challenging for a Grandma. The past participant photos and the promise of five slot canyons kept it at the top of my list. After running 56 road miles at Comrades it seemed like this might be my year to do it!

Vacation Races organized the race. They organize a dozen half marathons in different National Parks, along with ultra-marathons in Zion, Bryce & Antelope Canyon, and a running festival called Trailfest. Antelope Canyon Ultras offer several race distances; a half marathon on the runnable Page Rim Trail, a 55k which skips Antelope Canyon but includes Horseshoe Bend and Waterholes Canyon, a 50-mile, and a 100-mile race which follows the same course as the 50 but adds five more loops of the Page Rim Trail which you would run at night. If you want to run through Antelope Canyon, do the 50-mile or the 100-mile race.

I must confess to having a genuine feeling of fear the week before the race. Why the week before you might wonder? Because I ran the Monument Valley Half Marathon the weekend before with a 6,000' elevation and the same sandy conditions. It was tough, -really tough. It scared the sh-t out of me. It took me 2:40 to finish the race, and it exhausted me. I spent the rest of the week getting very little sleep.

After nightmares of my demise, I seriously considered dropping to the 55k. I sliced and diced my options, studied the 50-mile race cut-offs, developed my race pace plans, and played as much with my head as I could. Is this normal for me, not really, but I had

this persistent skeletal image of me out on the trail? I could not give up, I just had to run through Antelope Canyon...

Thankfully, Bob and I shared a table at a pre-race Italian dinner with a 100-mile runner from upstate New York (Russ). He settled my mind. It would be his first 100-miler and he was so confident, upbeat, and excited. How could I feel so nervous? I finally slept well that night, something I desperately needed.

At 5:45 am on the outskirts of Page, we prepared for the race start. It was pitch black and cold outside, but there was a traditional Indian hogan (a mud and log hut) with a central stove to keep us warm, sweet! Donning headlamps the 50-milers sprang forth at a crawl for the first mile, climbing up a stone ridge before we get on the sandy trail. Russ and the other 100-milers were right behind us at 6:00 am. We were a parade of headlamps across the desert.

The first leg of our race was the highly anticipated out and back section through Antelope Canyon. We head out on a sandy trail and drop into our first slot canyon, Owl Canyon before we get to the Antelope Canyon aid station at mile 5.3.

The initial pass through this aid station was the first of two Grim Reaper cut-off checkpoints, get through by 7:30 am or you get pulled off the course. The slogan was DON'T FEAR THE REAPER!

After the aid station, we followed the sand entry road down to the infamous Antelope Canyon. The canyon was glorious. You are in a sculptural cave. Everyone stops to take photos. It's exhilarating but went by so quickly!

From there it is up and over the rock to run above the canyon, back on the sand road, where I chatted briefly with a fellow Green Bay Packer fan, through the aid station and back through Owl Canyon. Three slot canyons in 11 miles in 2:20 and feeling good, certainly better than I did at Monument Valley. Running at 4,000' is much easier than 6,000'!

I plan to meet Bob at the Horseshoe Aid

station at mile 20.2. Between here and there is an aid station… and a whole lot of sandy trails. We are running on Navajo land used for grazing. Our trails are access roads for trucks to get across the land. We climbed three escarpments along the way. A well-deserved break from the sand!

Bob is at the aid station, aka, the runner's smorgasbord. The station is offering a wide array of food, drinks, medical assistance, and toilets. The organized runners can leave a drop bag that might contain socks, sunglasses, more food, extra clothes, medications, etc. The race hosts a spectator's shuttle from the start/finish line out to this aid station, so it was the only place we see our supporters.

Bob restocked my fuel bottle with my Hammer smoothie mix (Hammer gel and water) while I refilled my water flask and dumped the sand out of my shoes. The plan is for Bob to stay at the aid station while I run the 12.1-mile loop back to check in here.

At some point, Russ's pacer, Mike, and his wife, Brenda, will arrive. Mike would run 70 miles (through the night) to pace Russ and get him across the 100-mile finish. Mike received no medal or race credit for running 70 miles. Mike = saint in my book! The role of a pacer in ultra-distance races is immeasurable.

The Horseshoe Aid station is the second Grim Reaper checkpoint. I had to be there by 12:20 am, did it at 10:25 am! Here is a photo of the Grim Reaper with a 55k runner. They are using comedy to soften the blow. Luckily, this runner will claim a half marathon finish.

We run about a quarter-mile down to the edge of the cliff at the Colorado River... can you believe this? I held on tight to that post and did not look down. The brain goes on hold and I "just do it!

I wondered what slip rock trail surfaces meant? This is my trail. It's as rough as sandpaper! The pink flag at the shrub is a course

marker. They bring joy and reassurance when you find them... but it's much easier to follow Russ!

Below is the famous Horseshoe Bend, an entrenched meander. I looked forward to this section of the course, and the scenery did not disappoint. Everyone was stopping for selfies and to look over the edge. As you might see, the Colorado River takes a 180-degree turn here and the cliffs are 1200' or more above the river. It is the most visited spot in the area and for good cause! Luckily for me, I ran with Russ in my sights for a good portion of this section. Russ took the photo above.

The next highlight is crossing Highway 89 and dropping into Waterholes Canyon. The scramble down into the canyon was another one of those "holy cow" moments. We have run 27.5 miles and then must do some rock scrambling to descend, ouch!

The canyon floor required some light footwork. It was gorgeous inside the canyon and if you choose to do the 55k this is the one you traverse.

Do you see the pink flag trail marker in the following photo? I am not lost yet!

Then it is a three-mile desert crossing to get back to see Bob at the Horseshoe Aid station. I can feel my left toe throbbing and as often as I have stopped to shake out the sand from my shoe it is never often enough. The 50 milers have the option of stopping here and turning in their bibs to claim a 55k finish. This requires some quiet thinking on my part. I will have seen the most scenic parts of the course; the rest will be 5.5 more miles of sand and then 11 miles of the runnable Page Rim Trail. I believe I can finish 50 miles but at what physical cost?

I arrive at the aid station, the same drill... Bob prepares my Hammer smoothie bottle, I refill water, dump out the sand from my shoes, hit the toilet, and am then ready to go. Bob quickly asks if I have my Hammer smoothie bottle, no I don't? ~and the hunt begins?

I retrace my steps, twice, no bottle? I decide that this is a sign from a higher power, I need to turn in my bib to claim a 55k finish and I feel a sense of relief. Suddenly I hear my name. Bob runs over with my bottle in hand! OK, another sign from my higher power, so we quickly kiss and I am off to finish 50 miles.

The running does not last long since we have to run up this long sandy hill. I meet up with another gal and we have a chat. For the next 5.5 miles, we tag team in the desert. I run ahead, filling my shoes with sand, stop, empty my shoes, and then she passes me. I run ahead and pass her filling my shoes with sand again, stop, empty shoes, and repeat! After three miles I finally realize that I can make better

time by walking fast and not filling my shoes with sand! As my friend Julia says "Run when you can, walk when you have to!"

We hit even deeper sand and a steep climb up to the runnable Page Rim Trail (photo above). What joy, I can run again! Thirty-eight miles in and I am excited about running! I feel like I am going so fast yet it was a 12:00 pace. I passed so many walkers. I feel so good about my stamina!

Below is a photo of me coming into the Lake Powell Aid station, mile 43.2, and looking strong. I tell Bob that I can finish in daylight, shooting for 6:00 pm. The cut-off is 8:45 so I am in terrific shape and should place in my age group! ~Yah. My goal is to not let anyone pass me, so I play tag with another guy. He is run/walking and I am trying to stay at a steady pace. Each time he passes me he thanks me for motivating him, then he tuckers out and starts walking so I pass. He was great company for the last five miles!

I pass through the last aid station at mile 48.2. The volunteers are so supportive, one gentleman has been screaming motivational serenades to each runner as they depart the station. He has been going strong for hours and is the talk of the trail! ~ a contender for the best aid station award! I run through 1.5 miles of deep sand to get to the finish. I just want to knock this thing out so hustle along, filling my shoes with sand and enjoying every moment as the weight gets heavier and heavier!

It is up the catwalk through the natural stone amphitheater and the finish line! I did it! My smile is broad and deep! My time was 12:18:34, the prize was first in my age group, awesome! I see a few of my new friends at the finish line before heading over to the food table. I ran the race on 15 Hammer/Stinger gels so all I can focus on is the pizza van parked 100' from the finish line. ~How utterly perfect!

The sun set and we had our pizza boxes in hand. We drove out and quickly noted the runners crossing sign at the Page Rim Trail. There they were, the 100 milers! They still had five more loops of the Page Rim Trail before they could claim a belt buckle. I can honestly say that I was so happy to be going back for a shower, pizza, and a warm bed. We woke up feeling a profound sense of respect for Russ and Mike, who crossed the finish line around noon on Sunday (30 hours). ~R-E-S-P-E-C-T!

Chapter 30: Belfast Marathon

Date: May 5, 2019, 9 am, Belfast, Northern Ireland

Weather: Overcast, 39F start, 50F at the finish

Participation: 4,800 marathon, all events 19,000 runners

~So, you think you have heard it all? Read on my friend, read on….

Northern Ireland is easy to access from Cornwall, so we booked a long weekend and then started to develop a list of places to see. Bob and I are big Game of Thrones (GOT) fans. We read all the books and then watched the HBO TV series for years. It just so happens we are taking this trip during the final season and GOT mania has caught on like wildfire. Tourism numbers in Northern Ireland have skyrocketed and GOT gets most of the credit for it. We start our trip with a pilgrimage to see film locations outside Belfast along with another tourist hot spot, The Giants Causeway.

Here is the film site of the Dark Hedges, an ancient avenue of 240-year-old beech trees that lined The Kings Road in the GOT show. A fitting setting for a horse, cart, and a disguised Arya Stark.

Then on to see Dunluce Castle aka Castle Greyjoy; Larrybane Quarry, the location of the Renley Baratheon camp, and a key location if, like us, you are a fan of Brienne of Tarth; Ballintoy Harbor aka The Kingdom of Pike and the Iron Islands which is in the next photo. Next, we met the farmer that hosted the film crew at Dragonstone Cliffs, what a perfect name! He entertained us with stories of the action. Imagine you're standing on Ireland's tallest cliffs, which rise 600', suddenly Daenerys returns to Dragonstone on the back of Drogon, the dragon! ~glorious!

213

The marathon organizers ship your bibs before the race, so no expo. A great perk since we were away from Belfast trying to maximize our time sightseeing. We arrive in Belfast and went to the hotel to get organized. I lay out my running "ghost" or outfit to prepare for the next day's race, hat, shirt, shorts, calf sleeves, socks, shoes.... wait, where is the running bra?! Yikes, no bra, what am I to do?

It is 6 pm; I look up running stores, all closed at 6 pm. I look up department stores, one is in the area but after more research, I find they have no athletic department. Should I cancel my run? Should I get to a pharmacy and buy elastic bandages to wrap around my chest? I research running bra designs online. In retrospect, that seems desperate, but it settled me down. I will run in my daily underwire bra and tighten up every strap to lock the tissue in place. This race has a six-hour cut-off, so I will walk if I need to!

Race morning, we board the marathon bus from City Hall. The bus takes us through East Belfast, an area known as a stronghold for the Ulster Volunteer Force (UVF), and Ulster Defense Association (UDA), paramilitary loyalist organizations. Belfast is still a highly segregated city with divisions based on religion. They fill the city with political murals promoting the belief system of the local neighborhood. It's a place that requires some time to absorb and understand, so we vowed to do our best with our remaining time in Belfast. The divisiveness with an "in your face" attitude surprised me! I took a few photos of the Loyalist UVF and UDA murals we saw along the early course on Newtownards Road, East Belfast.

We arrive at our race start, Stormont, aka, Parliament House, home of the Northern Ireland Assembly. In 2017, the Northern Ireland Assembly collapsed because of a financial scandal with a renewable heating program. It's been two years and there is still no government. I  am in dismay; politics must be a tricky and frustrating business here??

We enter Bob in the 8-mile walk event. There are also options to run a half marathon or a marathon relay event. The weather was perfect and I am looking forward to seeing more of Belfast. This is a new course for the Belfast Marathon. It should be flatter and faster than in previous years and they changed the race to Sunday, and that has increased participation.

The course starts downhill and takes place on very wide streets so it does not feel crowded. I found the first mile or so a little numbing in the makeshift running bra, but after the second mile, I seemed to get used to it. By mile three, I am assessing the  murals. Faces covered, guns held high... "Wheresoever, howsoever or whenever we are called upon to make our exit, we shall do so as free men" UVF East Belfast.

Things seem to go well, but at mile five, I stumble and it quickly becomes a tumble. It is way too early in the race for this, and I doubt it bodes well for me. I pick myself up, dust off, and carry on. I seem to be OK, perhaps I am learning to land properly?

Mile 7, Ormeau Park, the home to our finish line. We go through the park and can see the finish and finally some spectators! We head for downtown Belfast, past the Gas Works, City Hall (see photo), The Fitzwilliam (our hotel), Crown Liquor Saloon, the hot spots, ~exciting!

Mile 10 and we see the largest sculpture in Belfast ahead called Rise. For me, it is appropriately named because I am ticking off some fast miles. I get to the half in 1:58, great given the challenges of the day. The next course highlight is Falls Road, the area of Belfast known for its Unionist and Catholic beliefs. The murals are known to be less about violence and more about human rights.

Next is the hill climb, a 200' climb over two miles. I keep running with

just a few short breaks towards the top of the hill. Then into Waterworks park and our first aid station with gels. I need a bit of a recharge; I want to take advantage of the downhill miles.

We head back to the downtown area to see the Big Fish sculpture on the River Langan. We run along the river and then the towpath, lovely. We see the finish in Ormeau Park on the other side of the towpath. My watch is showing 24 miles and a fast time of 3:34. We run past the park and keep going! It is a slight uphill and

I am feeling it. Then it's back downhill and finally into the park. I clock in at 4:01:42 and 26.86 miles. Some city runs show a longer distance and it frustrates my pacing.

Bob congratulates me on such a strong finish and rushes me to baggage pickup. We hopped in line for what became a one-hour wait! I had Bob to keep me warm, but too many others were shivering in a tank and shorts. There was a diverse spread of post-race food, but we left for our hotel to warm up.

We squeeze in a trip to the Game of Thrones Exhibition to see theatrical costumes, props, and memorabilia from the show. As a fan, I had to finish my big day seated on the Iron Throne!

Back at the hotel, I log in to check the race results. *"Approximately 460 additional meters were added to the officially measured course of 26.2 miles. This was due to human error, with the lead car diverting from the official route. In the meantime, we are in the process of adjusting runners' times to reflect the correct distance."*

My time of 4:01:42 became 3:58:36, so another sub 4:00 marathon! ~What an unforgettable day!!!

Chapter 31: Thunder Dragon Marathon

Date: May 26, 2019; 8:30 am, Paro, Bhutan

Weather: 60F at the start

Participants: 180 total runners with 75+ foreigners.

YAK DRUL, Land of the Thunder Dragon, Bhutan...

Bhutan or Yuk Drul, aka, Land of the Thunder Dragon, ranks #1 in the world for mean land elevation at 10,760'. It is a landlocked country in the Himalayan Mountains bordered by India and China. It is 1/4 the size of the state of New York with a population of 825,000. It has a national policy that requires 60% of the country to be under forest cover.

There are a few more key things to understand about Bhutan. The state religion is Buddhism. The country was ruled by a king since 1909 but moved towards its first democratic elections in 2008. Until 1974 Bhutan remained in complete isolation from foreigners, an intentional policy to preserve the national traditions. They have an intriguing development policy embedded in the constitution called Gross National Happiness (GNH). GNH is rooted in the principles of the country's religion, Buddhism, with its focus on compassion, contentment, and calmness. The sale of tobacco is banned throughout Bhutan. The country started TV broadcasts in 1999, the last country in the world to do so.

Bhutan is trying to modernize in a way that preserves the best of the country yet provides modern services to the people. It will be a difficult task and I so admire them for it.

Our Adventure...

Why did we choose to come to Bhutan? Bob and I wanted to visit Bhutan for our tenth anniversary but work schedules would not allow it. Back then we were hoping to hike during the alpine flower season in May. Luckily, I stumbled across the Marathon Tours-Bhutan Thunder Dragon Marathon trip. It was a combination of 4 days hiking on the Druk Path in May (peak rhododendron flowering), sightseeing in the towns of Paro and

Thimphu along with a marathon and half marathon in Paro, ~perfect for us!! We have never done tour group traveling before so went in with a little trepidation! Over the trip, we developed a great bond with everyone in our group and made several new friends!

The trip started with high-altitude hiking so we could acclimatize. We began with a 1,700' climb to visit the most photographed site in Bhutan, the Taktsang Monastery (Tigers Nest) at 10,000'. Why is this monastery built on the side of a remote mountain? Guru Rinpoche, who brought Buddhism to Bhutan, was carried to a cave below the current  monastery from Tibet on the back of a flying tigress. We heard some amazing stories on our visit, Guru Rinpoche was quite the personality!

Next, we spent four days on the Druk Path Trek, one of the most scenic high-altitude short treks in Bhutan. We followed a wilderness trail and saw species rhododendron flowering on the mountainside. Along the hike, we had sweeping views of valleys, lakes, and the Himalayan mountains. As we hiked back down the mountain, we trekked through the Phadjoding monastery. My favorite moment was watching the yak herders move the herds down the trail. Imagine hearing the bells echo in the mountain!

The evening before the race, all the international runners met up for dinner and an opportunity to pick up our bibs and t-shirts. We learned a little about the race history. The event started in 2007 with a small group from the UK. There was no running club in Bhutan, so the race organizers (Blue Poppy Tours) got some interest from the local military and some Bhutanese joined the race. It has grown over the years and the organizers have used it as a tool to further interest in running in Bhutan. The event is free for Bhutanese runners. Free transportation is provided from Thimphu (about an hour away). The Bhutanese runners are eligible

for financial prizes (the first-place prize is equal to the average yearly wage). Only Bhutanese men were eligible to run the marathon, they allowed no Bhutanese women because the interest from women was low and the finish times are slower than the men's times. To make the round-trip bus route from Thimphu and back in one day, runners must race aggressively. One day a Bhutanese woman will prove them wrong!

Here is the course profile for the race, starting at 7,800' and peaking at almost 8,400' at mile 18. This is not a race for a PR if you live at sea level.

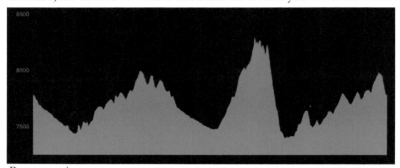

Race morning, our group walked down to the race start at Udumwara Resort. Leave your baggage anywhere in the race tent with no fear of theft, amazing! Local chanting monks blessed the race before the start, ensuring us good luck.

We all head off towards town,

spirits soaring! The half and full marathon start together at 8:30 and run along the same course for 8k/5 miles. Early on we look for the prayer flag festooned suspension bridge which takes us across the Paro River.

~It was amazing!

The first five miles are a gradual downhill on the road. I struggled to find the right pace, a 9:50 pace felt difficult?? I could feel my heart wanting to leap out of my chest. I can't run a marathon like this! I eventually settled into an 11:30 pace, still struggling on the uphill. Early on I started my mantra of "walk uphill, run downhill." The scenery certainly kept me distracted from the physical pain.

We ran along the Paro Chu River to its convergence with the Wang Chu, then ran along the Wang Chu River. Once out of town I see the rice paddy fields. It is planting time and people are setting rice plants in place.

At 11k/6.8 miles we run on a wide trail, not technical but it is a constant

uphill from mile 5 until mile 10 so it takes its toll. Looking down into the valley, the rice paddies fade into the overall view of the full Paro Valley.

We are headed to a short out and back section at 16k/10 miles. The volunteers will stamp our hand as proof that we did not cut the course (key for the Bhutanese after the prizes!). I am running with Bhutanese men around me. I keep seeing our Marathon Tours guide, Jeff, which is terrific and accounts for some of my better  pictures. I feel good at this point and got word that I was second or third female!

I could maintain an 11:00 minute pace until we started the BIG uphill climb at 26k/16 miles. It was straight-up switchbacks on a rough dirt road, no shade, and the full sun affected me. Everyone walked up the hill and my lap pace dropped to a 20:00 minute mile; crazy, but it's too steep.

At 28k/17.5 miles we entered the single-track trail portion of the race. They say what goes up must come down and down it did. We dropped 800' in a mile on a technical trail with rocks painted yellow to help spot them. Volunteers whistled to each other to mark our passing from point to point. The air was perfectly still on the mountaintop and the heat was draining. They set up signs to sharpen our tenacity. This one says, "Don't

just run the race, take pleasure in being in it." ~Only a donkey ride could be more welcome than this sign!

One highlight of the race is running past the Paro Dzong (monastery) and over the bridge that spans from the Dzong to the town.

One of my concerns was the prevalence of semi-feral dogs. They roam everywhere. Would the local sport be heel nipping? My concerns were ill-founded; they laid about, soaking in the sun, and harmless. Just as unassuming were my road-sharing companions, the local cows.

For me, the course news gets worse from here. The next flat portion of the course was impossible for me to "run." My heart was just working too hard. Had I done a little more research before the race, I would have known to eat more than three gels (I was running for fun so not in race mode), drink much more water, and regulate my pace early in the race. I now ran when I felt good and walked when it felt right. The volunteers had bananas and water, but after sitting in the sun neither had much allure. Several runners overtook me in the last few miles of the race. I did not care, ~imagine that!

I got my mojo back when I saw friends seated outside our hotel, I knew it was the beginning of a long downhill and I was close to the finish, full-on running commenced. I felt ill crossing the finish line and was glad to find shade and the cool lobby of the resort!

I earned three Marathon Globetrotter flags today! This is my 30th country so I will celebrate! Post-race we enjoyed a nice lunch at the resort before meandering back up to shower, rehydrate and relax at our hotel.

~Am I glad I did the marathon distance? yes! I loved the scenery but had a few cross words for the racecourse designers. I should have done much more research on high altitude running but now I know...

Bhutan has the highest mean elevation in the world, 10,670'. Post-race I learned from Runners World that high altitude training happens at 5,000'. I run an easy 9:30 pace at sea level but need to adjust to 10:30/11:00 at

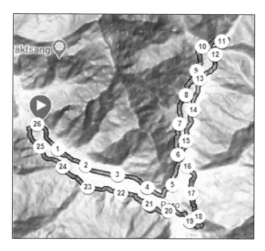

5,000'. No wonder I was struggling so much! ~I was running between 7,800' and 8,400'.

At 6,000' I exhale and perspire twice as much moisture as I do at sea level. I did not drink enough and should have carried water with me like I normally do!

The first impediment to running at altitude is the drop in the oxygen content of the blood. Because of the reduced air pressure at higher altitudes, oxygen diffuses into the red blood cells slower. This drop in blood oxygenation corresponds with a drop in VO2 max, a direct measurement of the oxygen absorbed by the body during exercise. For every thousand feet of elevation increase over 1,000 feet above sea level, VO2 max drops by 1.9%. My VO2 max would drop almost 15%! ~Wow, no wonder it felt so difficult. It wasn't just a lack of fuel and water; I had no oxygen in my blood, I was physically struggling!

Post-race we relaxed in one of Bhutan's unique hot stone baths, a form of traditional Bhutanese medicine where fresh river water is mixed with local artemisia leaves and heated with fire-roasted river stones. The stones are heated in an open fire and deposited into a chamber of the wooden tub. As the hot stone hits the cool water the stones crack, releasing high concentrations of minerals, it was exactly what my body craved after days of hiking and running.

Archery is the national sport of Bhutan, and the archers take great pride in the sport. On the next page is an example of the local archery team practicing at the Archery Grounds in Paro. It is quite entertaining to see them on the archery ground standing at a distance of over 100 meters to shoot the target. The archers are wearing the national dress, required at all Bhutan government buildings, schools, and formal occasions which is the gho for men and the kira for women. Our guides wore them daily, except for race day!

While waiting for the rest of the group to enjoy the hot stone baths, I was given an archery lesson. ~Like me, this trip hit the target!

Chapter 32: Race to The Stones

Date: July 13 & 14, 2019, 7:30 am, Lewknor, UK

Weather: partly sunny, 58F at the start, 73F high

Participation: 730 finishers 50K/50K and 1123 finishers for 100K

We Believe More is in you......

Race to the Stones is a 100k race that follows the historic Ridgeway Trail past Wayland's Smithy, Uffington, White Horse, and Barbury Castle before reaching the iconic ancient Stone Circle at Avebury. It is described as Britain's oldest road and is one of fifteen UK National Trails. For at least 5,000 years travelers have used the route as a reliable trading road to the Dorset coast and The Wash in Norfolk.

I dropped a huge rock on my foot two days before Race to the Stones. What is huge? ~14"x8"x3". The rock cut through a vein on the top of the foot; I lost over a cup of blood. I was crushed, I wouldn't be able to run! Drop a stone on your foot before the Race to the Stones, how ironic! My foot was swollen and throbbing on Thursday evening. Friday morning it started to look much better, less swelling but heavily bruised. I became hopeful, so Bob and I made the drive to the historic market town of Wallingford to have a lovely Italian meal and an evening's rest.

I decided Friday night to try running on Saturday and if it was too painful, I would spend Sunday with the family. Jess and Josie were scheduled to join us late Saturday. Sunday the family would be out looking at dollhouses and butterflies, so by running I was missing their fun!

Saturday morning, I went to the race start and tentatively got my bearings. Bob and I had a plan; I would see him at mile 3 to let him know how I was feeling. Off I go.... Three miles later, as I saw him... tripped.... and my confidence eroded! It was just a grazing of the knee, so I shook it off and carried on, but Bob looked concerned.

On day 1, I was most looking forward to a 3-mile section of the trail called Grimm's Ditch at mile 9.5. They speculate that it is an ancient boundary separated by a ditch. It was a run through spectacular woods.

Then it's a 2-mile downhill run to the Thames River and then 3-miles of flat running as we meander along the river to the towns of Goring and Streatley. Past the town, we run a long uphill on local roads, and then at mile 21, we are back on scenic trails to the finish.

The Ridgeway Trail takes us through a series of farm fields, dubbed the "Field of Dreams." It is epic, running with your arms out letting the wheat ears slap your hands.

I did quite well. I was still running when I arrived at the Day 1 finish line. I went immediately to the medical tent. The doctor gave my foot a good look and said if I could keep the swelling down overnight, I could run the next day. That was what I needed to hear, YAH!

On day 2, my foot felt even better! My body responds better than most to these back-to-back races. The weather is similar to yesterday, overcast and not too hot. Like Race to the Tower, the second day is a casual start, go out when you are ready. I try to get out before the walkers. Once on the trail, I find that it's wide enough and there is plenty of room to pass the walkers.

There are a few race highlights early on Day 2, Uffington Castle, the White Horse, and Wayland's Smithy. Uffington Castle and the White Horse are at mile 8 with

access to the castle right off the Ridgeway. The castle is from the iron age. Much to my surprise, it is a ditch and a huge mound of dirt. It has impressive views and you can see for

miles! I have seen the White Horse from the train window on our trips to Polperro so was looking forward to seeing it here but it is on the other side of the fort and not visible from the Ridgeway Trail. In the past, the prehistoric horse was scoured during a local festival to keep it visible, but it is now maintained by the National Trust.

The Wayland's Smithy is a Neolithic tomb built just off the Ridgeway in a field at mile 9. I did not stop to have a look but it was well signed and is a destination for many walkers on the trail. We went inside several similar tombs in Ireland.

This course seems much more runnable than Race to the Stones, there are plenty of hills but the footing on the chalk is much better unless you have ruts. It can be difficult after a season of rain, but for us, it is terrific underfoot.

Mile 15, completion of another hill climb to Liddington Castle, another iron age castle site with ditches, earth mounds, and a beautiful view of the countryside. We stay along the ridge until mile 20, where we drop down to the village of Osbourne St. George. Then back up again to the finest iron age fort on our route, Barbury Castle, at mile 24. The Ridgeway Trail runs right through the middle of the earthworks. The distant views are gorgeous on The Ridgeway Trail.

We stay on top of the ridge for another 3 miles and then start

the long downhill run to the great stone henge and circles of Avebury. English Heritage describes it as "one of the greatest marvels of prehistoric Britain. Built and much altered during the Neolithic period, roughly between 2850 BC and 2200 BC, the henge survives as a huge circular bank and ditch, encircling an area that includes part of Avebury village.

Within the henge is the largest stone circle in Britain - originally about 100 stones - which in turn encloses two smaller stone circles." We ran down the road at the upper right-hand side of the photo, past the circular banks into the northern circle to The Cove or the Devil's Brandirons.

~What a photo!!!!!

Then it is back up the village and a race

through the cornfield to get to the finish line. I was determined to pass a few competitors through the cornfield and made a sprint to the finish!

I was glowing when I crossed the finish line!! I found out I was first in my age group! But the family was missing? I wanted them to see my inspiring sprint finish on an injured foot!! I quickly learned that the butterfly park down the road was much more fun than watching Grandma running through a circle of stones. We did not stay long in Avebury, we had dollhouse furniture and a butterfly garden to show silly running Grandma!

Chapter 33: Arches Ultra-50K

Date: January 25, 2020, 8:00 start, Moab, Utah, USA

Weather: Overcast, 28F at the start, high of 32F

Starting elevation: 4,579 feet, Total ascent: 2,500 feet

Trail Running amongst The Holy Land and finishing up the "Big Five" of Utah...

Utah is state #38 in my 50-state quest and race #96 in my goal to reach 100 marathons. Utah could be an opportunity to see more National Parks; Moab is a base for two of the best, Arches and Canyonlands. With a little research, I found we could string together Natural Bridges National Monument, the upper reaches of Glen Canyon National Recreation Area, Grand Staircase-Escalante National Monument, and Capitol Reef National Park while traveling along some of our most memorable scenic byways. Couple that with a four-wheel-drive vehicle and the trip would be breathtaking.

Moab, population 5,300, is a mountain bike, trail running, and rock-climbing mecca. Late January might not seem like the right time to sign up for a 50K trail race, but the inaugural event in 2019 offered a gallery of pictures with azure skies and scenic vistas. 2020 was a new day, and I doubt they will post our snowy race photos. Running on packed snow is easier than loose sand. I found this race much easier than the deep sandy trails of Antelope Canyon. -no regrets.

We planned to fly to Denver and then fly United to Moab. Little did we know that the pilot needs 800' of visibility below the clouds to land safely. The week of our travel, none of the flights had that. Our flight circled the runway in Moab, had a quick look, and went right back to Denver.

~Oh my, what to do? Stay over and risk a flight the next day or drive six hours from Denver to Moab? Saint Bob was adamant that we drive so I would not miss the race!

We spent our first day in Moab up at "The Holy Land" alias Arches National Park. We had good visibility until we got to the upper section of the park. We hiked out to Delicate Arch, it's on every license plate in Utah and was the graphic for our race. Our favorite arch, Landscape Arch, was deep in the park, in the snowier reaches of the Devils Garden; the 300-foot span of varnished desert rock looks stunning against the low cloud cover and snowy ground:

Saturday, January 25, race day; The Arches 50K course follows the Bar M, Klonzo, and Klondike mountain bike trails just west of the boundary of Arches National Park. Unfortunately, we had low cloud cover again so no breath-taking views. With snow-covered trails, I fixed my eyes on the terrain, safety first! The next photo is from the Klonzo Aid station, close to the Fiery Furnace area of Arches.

Because of the muddy conditions, the race organizers changed the first section of the race to minimize critical trail damage. When runners go through deep mud or run off-trail race organizers must restore the damage. The organizers repaired ten miles of trails at another event and did not want a repeat of that experience. Our 31-mile race became a 29-mile race, but after spending six hours running in snow and mud, I was very pleased to finish the shorter distance!

I was nervous after a winter with not as much training as I would like. We started the race on a road to spread out the pack, then reached the single-track trail. It was not as slippery as I expected, and my new Altra

trail shoes worked out perfectly! I saw Bob at the Bar M aid station; this is my approach.

Unfortunately, I hit the 15-mile aid station early due to the change in the course so Bob hadn't arrived yet. The next ten miles offered more slick rock, muddy hill descents, and thicker snow coverage. I was giddy to see Bob at mile 26, a marathon done and only another 5 miles to go. This is a photo of the typical aid station smorgasbord, the muddy red sand, and the variety in dress. Yes, that runner is in shorts!

On the home stretch, I took my only faceplant! No blood was drawn, but I garnered much awe for toughness at the finish line.

By midafternoon the clouds rose and we had much better views, ~a great distraction as we ran back on access roads!

I crossed the finish with a time of 5:55:57 and 3rd of 11 women in the age group 50-59, excited with that! Mad Moose served up post-race enchiladas, hot coffee, and snacks but we were anxious to get back to Moab for real food and a shower!

The race was well run, and I encourage everyone to look at the entire series of races offered by Mad Moose events. They

have several races in and around Moab, Bears Ears, and Canyonlands along with numerous races in the Pikes Peak, Colorado Springs area.

Post-race we explored Canyonlands National Park, which is vast, 527 square miles carved up by the Green and Colorado rivers with three distinct regions; The Isle in the Sky has tremendous views from the top of the mesas into the canyons, The Needles District with hiking trails through an area of rocky needle formations and The Maze District. A runner on the Chesler Park/Needles trail passed us! I missed an opportunity for a great trail run!

Here is a photo from The Needles hike:

And a photo from Mesa Arch at The Isle in the Sky:

We found more stone bridges at Natural Bridges National Monument. Only one trail was safe for us to hike, but it made for a great early stop on

our drive along the scenic Bicentennial Highway to the Upper reaches of Glen Canyon Recreation Area. The 360-degree views were spectacular.

We carried on to the unpaved Notom-Bullfrog Road to reach Capitol Reef National Park. Capitol Reef is a less-known park that is highly prized for its geology and wildlife. Capitol Reef preserves a 75-mile section of the Water Pocket Fold, a warp in the earth's surface with a rock wrinkle jutting straight up into the air. Our goal was the Burr Trail Switchbacks (4-wheel drive required!) one of the few places where you can drive through the fold. A picture is worth a thousand words, and this icy drive left us happily speechless!

We followed the Burr trail to Boulder, UT so we could drive through the northernmost section of the Escalante National Monument. The section

adjacent to Capitol Reef is part of the unfortunate 2017 proposed downsizing of the park to allow for the mining of coal, oil, gas, and tar sands. We are looking towards the red cliffs, ~spectacular! I shudder to think that this section of the Burr Trail could be tarnished with development and mining.

Then into the easternmost section of snowy Dixie National Forest with a stop at the Wildcat Visitor Center before heading to the more accessible center of Capitol Reef National Park. From the scenic viewpoint at Dixie Forest, we can see Capitol Reef and the Water Pocket Fold and, in the distance, the La Sal Mountains beyond Moab.

The Mormons settled in and around Capitol Reef and turned the land adjacent to the Fremont River into orchards. The orchards are still in production and as a park visitor in the fall you can help yourself. In winter, we enjoyed the wildlife, had our first sighting of a kit fox and bighorn sheep. The paved scenic drive to Capitol Gorge, an area within the park, is framed by red cliffs.

Bob and I left Utah as huge supporters of the "Mighty Five" campaign. Utah's program to encourage visits to Zion, Bryce, Capitol Reef, Canyonlands, and Arches. We did some epic trail runs in Zion, Bryce, and the Grand Canyon with Vacation Races several years ago. So many opportunities to create a running holiday and support our national parks along the way! Get out there, hit the trails, and enjoy!

Chapter 34: 2020 Publix Atlanta Marathon

Date: March 1, 2020, 7:00 am, Atlanta, Georgia, USA

Weather: Overcast, 33F at start, high of 58F

Participation: 2112 marathoners, 11,150 for all distances

The 2020 Olympic Team Trials-Marathon, Bridesmaid Reunions, and 62 Hills...

The 2020 Olympic Team Trials for the marathon were on leap year Saturday and the Publix Atlanta Marathon, Half Marathon, and 5K were Sunday. Tracie, from our 1991 Team Disquick (ultimate Frisbee) is living in Atlanta. Mary, also from the team, drove down from Virginia to spend the weekend with her...the makings of a great reunion. Add to that more friends, my NewRo running mates Mara and Melissa plus my massage therapist, Julia, and this had the makings of an epic weekend!

 Tracie and I were bridesmaids for Mary; the three musketeers! We three gals met through the ultimate Frisbee community and became very fast friends. We started in the local league but quickly joined the women's traveling team, eventually forming Team Disquick. We spent many a weekend playing tournaments up and down the east coast.

Bob and I came into town on Thursday and started to take in some of the Atlanta sites, The Sweet Auburn Market for lunch, The Martin Luther King, Jr. National Historical Park, Oaklands Cemetery, and the race expo.

Friday was spent seeing the Jim Henson puppet collection at the Center for Puppetry Arts, The Cocoa-Cola tour, and the National Center for Civil and Human Rights before the long-awaited reunion and dinner with Tracie and Mary.

On Saturday Melissa, Bob, and I went to the marathon trials at Centennial Olympic Park, the site of the 1996 bombing. The men were first on the start block at 12:08 pm and the energy was electric! At 12:20 pm the women went out, even more stirring since the number of women running seemed double the men's race!

As soon as the runners crossed the start the spectators fanned out to claim spots for cheering. The course was three loops on Peachtree Street and we were headed to the bridge over I-85 to see them pass by six times.

The best crowd response came for two pregnant women running the race. The applause was so loud that you could not hear each other talk. We all welled up with pride for how far woman's running has come. It was as recent as 1967 that Katherine Switzer had to run as KV Switzer, #261, to sneak into the Boston Marathon as an official entrant.

I found out later that both women, Rachel Hyland (27 weeks) and Lauren Philbrook (33 weeks) were track and cross-country teammates at Williams College. Our nephew, Cal, participated in track at Williams while Lauren Philbrook was back as a track coach in 2017/18, lucky Cal!

199 men signed up to race and 175 made it across the finish line; 425 women signed up and 390 crossed the finish. Such an immense field of women! The runners had sunshine, loads of brutal hills, and 20mph wind to contend with. Their performance was inspiring!

Sunday race day! I walked over to the start with Mara and Julia. I would run with Julia, who plans a 10:17 pace as practice for her upcoming pacing commitments. We haven't run side by side since the Ladies First Half in 2017, so I am super excited! I plan to stay with her to mile 13.1 and then hopefully to mile 21 for some photos with our cheer team of Mary, Tracie, Jeff, and Bob.

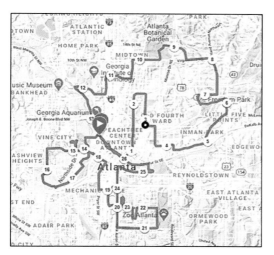

At the course review, I learned that the half marathon has 23 hills and the toughest hill of the course is between miles 10 and 12. There was no discussion of the second half, but the course profile shows that after mile 21 it is a slow uphill with lots of rolling hills along the way, so I'm nervous. Tracie and Jeff have armed me with some knowledge of the course scenery, so I looked forward to sightseeing through Atlanta, eating hills for breakfast!

The race starts along Centennial Olympic Park and heads through the downtown to Georgia State University and then north into the Old Fourth Ward. Early on, Julia spotted Kinnear, her husband's best man. We learned that Jennifer, another one of Julia's bridesmaids, was just a block behind us. Let the search begin! ~I ran back several blocks but couldn't find her.

By mile 4 we are into the heart of the Sweet Auburn District running right through the Martin Luther King, Jr. National Historical Park! We ran past Ebenezer Church, the MLK birth home, and the National Park Service restored houses along Auburn Avenue. What a great way to start a race!

~Even better when Julia finds Jennifer, and she joins us.

By mile 5 we were on Euclid Avenue in the heart of the Inman Park neighborhood, the first leafy suburb of Atlanta, conceived in 1886 and filled with lovely Victorian mansions. In 1973 they added it to the National Register of Historic Places as an example of the typical late 19th-century picturesque suburb, gorgeous and so close to downtown. They nailed picturesque!

I am keen to see the commercial area of Inman Park, Little Five Points, or L5P at mile 6. Tracie pointed it out as an area holding on to its alternative, counter-culture attitude. We had not been there but were told it was reminiscent of bohemian Haight Ashbury in San Francisco. It was everything she said and more, lots of hand-painted murals covered buildings with vintage shops, restaurants, junk shops, bars, tattoo shops. Here is an example:

Then it is on to Freedom Park and the Jimmy Carter Library at miles 6-7. Freedom Park is the largest city park in Atlanta and the Jimmy Carter Library sits in the middle of it. It is wonderful to see a glimpse of the library since we did not plan to get out here during our visit. For anyone interested, they have a great virtual tour online.

Miles 7-9 takes us through another residential neighborhood called Virginia Highland, it is adjacent to Inman Park with lovely smaller scale bungalows and wide leafy streets. At this point in the race, I was looking forward to miles 9-10 where we enter the famous Piedmont Park. We spent an afternoon there, visiting the orchid show at the Atlanta Botanical Garden with our friends. The racecourse took us into the southern corner, a lovely run along the lake but I wish we had seen more!

We very quickly entered the Mid-Town area, known for its mix of high-rise buildings and great restaurants but the highlight was running down 10th Street and crossing Piedmont Avenue to see the rainbow crosswalks. They were permanently installed in 2017 to mark the anniversary of the

Pulse nightclub shooting in Florida after a temporary installation in 2015 for the local pride festivities. Why Midtown? -because it is the epicenter of the Atlanta LBGTQ culture.

Two more blocks and we turn on Jupiter and are in a high-rise area, strange zoning, but Atlanta is known for spreading its development out to nodes around the city. We head to the campus of Georgia Tech to rub shoulders with the engineers for miles 11-12 before running down Marietta Street and back to the Olympic Centennial Park to drop off all the half marathon runners.

I was concerned, over 6,000 runners chose the half marathon and 2,000 chose the full, would we marathoners feel like second-class citizens? The first half of the course was stunningly scenic, so I was sure the second half could not compare. Julia, Jennifer, and I had stuck together and I was so happy to have them coming along for the back half!

We did a big loop on the wide streets around the Mercedes Benz Stadium, home to the Atlanta Falcons basketball team and the Atlanta United soccer team. This stadium replaced the famous Georgia Dome, which was imploded in 2018. More exciting to me was the upcoming Atlantic University Center southwest of downtown; the home of numerous historically black colleges.

At mile 15 we run through the campus of Morris Brown College, founded in 1881 by and for black students. Sadly, it has had some trouble since it lost its accreditation in 2002 due to a scheme to embezzle federal grants. On an up note, the school is back from bankruptcy and seems to be thriving again. Then through Clark Atlanta University, popular for its radio and television programs, ~movie director, Spike Lee attended classes there. The campus has been the backdrop for several films. It reminds me of the style at UVA, brick colonial. By mile 16 we have entered the campus of Spelman College, the oldest historically black college for women; the author Alice Walker is an alumna. Adjacent to it we see Morehouse College, a historically black college for men; it too has a long list of famous graduates including Martin Luther King, Jr., Spike Lee, and actor Samuel L. Jackson.

As we leave the campus area, Julia and I enter Castleberry Hill, an old red-light district and now a historic warehouse area filled with lofts, galleries, and most unusually a location for movie filming! If we get back to Atlanta, I will be doing one of the local movie set tours! Unfortunately, we lost Jennifer on the rolling hills and Julia is starting to feel the miles.

We run under I-20 and I-85 at mile 19 to see the original Olympic Stadium, which became Turner Field, home of the Atlanta Braves until 2016 when they moved to a new stadium north of the city. Now it is known as the Georgia State Stadium.

We run alongside the Olympic Cauldron Tower, which sits amongst a sea of parking lots. It was lit again yesterday for the duration of the Olympic trials. I remember when Muhammad Ali, suffering from Parkinson's Disease, lit the flame during the Opening Ceremonies for the 1996 Games in Atlanta.

I ran ahead of Julia, hoping to bank a little time for a visit with my spectator crew at mile 21. They met for breakfast and I would see them at

the 21-mile aid station. Right on cue, I see Bob, Mary, Tracie, and Jeff; gosh, what an energy boost they give me! They are all smiles and hugs and have made some cheer signs, so cool! I hang out hoping Julia and Jennifer would arrive, but after 4 minutes of waiting....no luck.

At mile-22, we enter Cheney Stadium at Phoenix Park, the recently renovated warm-up track for the 1996 Olympics. We do a lap of the track and then run alongside it on the street, I see Jennifer again and learn that Julia is not far behind, yah! She encourages me to run strong and I feel good so pick up the pace.

It was starting to get quite warm on the course as we continued up Capitol Avenue to see the Georgia State Capitol and then down Martin

Luther King, Jr. Drive to run alongside Oakland Cemetery… familiar territory as Bob and I had walked through the stately grounds on Thursday. The daffodils were out and the cemetery was unlike any I had seen before with outdoor patio tables and chairs set up amongst the grave sights… yes it was that picturesque!

Mile 24 and Bob unexpectedly yells my name! I pull to the side for a quick chat. He cheered for Julia at mile 21 and then walked over to see me again! What a great spectator. I tell him I am feeling great, will finish less than 4:30. A hug and I'm off.

Mile 25.5 and I still feel really strong, the count is up to 60 hills now and I am still running, no walk breaks at all except my 4-minute rest at mile 21. I set my sights on the 4:30 pacers that have been ahead of me since mile 21 and go for it. I passed them just as we hit Centennial Park on the same finish line that the Olympic hopefuls crossed the day before!

I had a fabulous day, Julia kept me chatting, Tracie had me well prepared to enjoy all the Atlanta neighborhoods and my 21-mile cheer squad of Bob, Mary, Tracie, and Jeff kept me highly motivated. I loved this race, hills and all!

Chapter 35: Covid-19 Puts the Brakes On

Covid-19 originated in China and very quickly left its impact on the world. I heard very little about it until the week before the February 17th announcement that only elites would be able to run the Tokyo Marathon on March 1st. We didn't understand just how contagious the virus was so we were surprised by the announcement. I had several friends scheduled to run the Tokyo race; they were forced to cancel dream vacations and scrambled to find alternate races. Who wants to waste four months of marathon training!

In the USA races were proceeding, Bob and I joined a group of friends in Atlanta for the March 1st Olympic Marathon Trials and Marathon. We thought that the 2020 Olympics would proceed! On the weekend of March 7/8, my friend was able to run the LA Marathon instead of Tokyo. It was the last of the major marathon events to go forward before racing came to a standstill.

Bob and I returned from Atlanta to our home in New York late on Monday, March 2nd. On March 3rd there was news that a local man from the neighborhood was quite ill from coronavirus. Bob and I were surprised since we assumed that an outbreak of the virus would start on the West Coast and creep across the country.

The crisis escalated quickly, by Friday our local case count was up to 160 people with over 1,000 people in quarantine. On March 10th, one week after we returned from Atlanta, New York state put in place a one-mile radius "containment zone" around our local synagogue. We live only a half-mile from the synagogue so we were now in the epicenter of the outbreak on the East Coast. Schools, houses of worship, and large gatherings within the containment zone were closed. We were told to wash our hands as we reenter your home, don't touch your face, and use hand sanitizer before entering your car, a store, etc.

By March 12th our governor announced that there would be no gatherings larger than 500 people in the state, four days later the gatherings were reduced to 50 people and all schools were closed. Movie theaters, gyms, casinos, and restaurant dining areas were all closed on March 18th. On March 20th, New York State announced NY State on Pause, all nonessential businesses were closed as confirmed coronavirus cases reached 7100. In two weeks, our world came to an unimaginable halt!

Friday, the 13th a harbinger of bad luck... I was scheduled to run the Boston Marathon on April 20, 2020, as marathon #98 but on Friday, March 13th they announced a postponement to September 14, 2020. Later in the day, The London Marathon, my 99th marathon, announced the postponement of their race from April 26 to October 4th, 2020. A black day for me indeed! I hoped for small-scale local trail marathons to replace these events, but as the coronavirus cases mounted, even the small trail events were canceled or postponed.

The state was in a race to slow the spread of the virus to ensure that those needing emergency services would be able to get help. April was horrific as the death toll climbed to 800 deaths per day in New York state, infections mounted and Zoom conference calls replaced our social life as people continued to self-isolate.

Thankfully, our governor encouraged running and hiking as a safe means to exercise. There would be no more group runs, but we could run on our own. Face coverings became the norm as you passed others out on the trails. I had a few weeks of withdrawal as they canceled my numerous social group runs. I started exploring the local trails for my long runs, which was very gratifying. I could eventually meet up with a few trail runners during the week, which was a mental lifeline. My group speed sessions continued at a much smaller scale until the local track closed in late March, then we moved to hill training on the local streets.

I had planned my 100th marathon to be on August 8th in Cornwall, UK at the RAT Race, an ultra I had done the two previous years. We had a fabulous group of over a dozen friends coming from the US to participate in the race and celebrate. The UK Looe Pioneers had a sizeable group signed up. The family was planning to field a few runners! I kept a deep-seated hope that as a smaller trail race in August it would go forward. I thought the virus would run out of opportunities to infect. With social distancing and face coverings stopping the spread, my race could go forward.... maybe it wouldn't be my 100th marathon but we would celebrate anyway. That was my hope, but on May 31st my hopes were dashed as the race director announced the race cancellation. He was sure they could not find 275 volunteers to assist with the event.

Friends had lost family members, so it was difficult to allow myself the opportunity to feel the disappointment I had for my situation. In the context of our surroundings, we were very lucky, but it did make me think very deeply about my 100-marathon goal. Should I take a break now? Should I allow my body to rest from the constant training? If I do take a break what will I do? I know that as a young mom I always wanted to be that woman who was able to stick to a regular exercise plan, but I never did that until I became a runner. I found that I need a consistent weekly schedule, my body functions better, my mind is clearer and I have an innate sense of pride in my chosen lifestyle.

I decided to stay on the lookout for very small trail races, they seemed to have the best chance of moving ahead. I continued speed work or hill training on Tuesdays, trail runs on Wednesdays, tempo runs on Thursdays, more trail running on Saturdays, and a long 15-20 mile run on Sundays all through March, April, May, June, and July.

Our scheduled flight to the UK in April was canceled; President Trump was not allowing British citizens to enter the USA so our airline canceled all its US flights. We had no choice but to postpone our yearly April trip to be with our family in the UK. In early June both New York State and the United Kingdom were seeing a sustained drop in the infection rate. We booked a new flight and with much trepidation, we went to London. The terminal was eerily vacant except for our flight, the plane left middle seats vacant and we all wore masks (kn95 mask and a face shield for us).

We settled in London, wore our face masks constantly, and isolated. I started searching for small UK trail races. I found some options, races that said they were moving forward with a small field, signed up, and had them postponed right before the race. Eventually, I found a race that looked promising, the Round Reading Ultra Marathon (RRUM). It had a really strong race plan for minimizing the spread of coronavirus. I was sure that this would be the one to kick start racing for me!

Chapter 36: Round Reading Ultra Marathon

Date: August 1, 2020, 7:00-9:00 am start, Reading UK

Weather: Overcast and cloudy, 33F at start, high of 58F

Participation: 258 finishers

This is the first official post Covid-19 lockdown race in the UK! What is the new Covid-19 race experience going to be like????

I went into this race with so many mixed emotions, excitement to be back racing, nervous about the public perception, concern about my ability to complete 50k, and hope that perhaps we turned a corner against Covid-19. The plan for race day was for the family to drive me to the race start at the Berkshire County Sports Club. They would see me start and finish. They would go to a local zoo during the race, their first outing since the UK lockdown started in late March.

As the first official UK ultra during the pandemic, this race had a strong Covid-19 plan. The first big change was the race start. We left in two-minute increments in groups of six people between 7-9 am. I had to submit three start time options; they awarded me 8 am. We arrived at the sports club and the impact of Covid-19 was quite apparent. The mood seemed tentative, the people extremely cautious, but the race volunteers and organizers were very enthusiastic.

The first stop was the spotless porta-potty with filled hand sanitizer. The second stop was bib pick-up. I mask up, use the hand sanitizer and with no queue, I complete my bib pick up. Due to Covid-19, they encouraged us to pack our own nutrition, which the race organizers would drop off at any aid station on the course. I packed two small bags with gel and electrolyte pills for aid stations #3 and #4. Then I was off to pick up the swag, which was a buff to use as a face covering when social distancing was not possible during the race. Welcome to the new normal??

At the race start, the officials grouped us in a block of six runners based on our bib number. They called our block up about ten minutes before our start time. We entered a roped-off square, three in front, and three in back. As they released each group, we crossed over to the square in front of us. I could only run solo or with members of my  group of six. I ran a few miles with Georgia from Hungary; we had similar pace and race strategies.

The town of Reading has a population of 250,000. Its economy was historically famous for the three B's, beer (Simonds Brewery), bulbs (Sutton Seeds), and biscuits (Huntley Palmer Biscuits). More recently the city has sent us some famous people including our granddaughter's favorite, Mr. Tumble, the comedian Ricky Gervais and of course Kate Middleton, Duchess of Cambridge, who was born in Reading.

The racecourse was literally a run around Reading. We started on the Thames Canal towpath and would run 50K (31 miles) around the perimeter of Reading through urban green spaces and woodland paths with a few streets thrown in to connect the various paths. The surface would be 20% paved and 80% trail but not technical. I had never spent time in Reading nor had the family, so it was all new territory.

I went into this race with hamstring tendinosis. The long runs, months of hill training, and the change to flat speed work in June were too much for my left leg. The connective tissue from the buttock right down to the knee was causing me pain the entire month of July. I cut back my speed and distance to allow it to heal. My goal for this race was to finish without further injury.

For the first six miles, we ran

the Thames Towpath. It was flat and incredibly scenic. The Thames Path is a 184-mile national long-distance path that starts at the Thames source in Kemble and ends at the Thames Barrier in Charleton in SE London. The Caversham Lock, in the photo, is on the Thames Path below the start of another canal, the Kennet and Avon Canal. It is a vibrant and especially scenic area.

We reach the first aid station at mile 6. The aid stations were self-serve; mask up, step to the table, sanitize your hands, help yourself to water (no electrolyte drink) and snacks in small cups, sanitize your hands and move on, all as quickly as possible. There was a cut-off here at 10:55 am, no problem for me! My leg was tight but OK so far.

We left the Thames Path and went up to the Tilehurst train station to the

streets of Purley. It's the start of the 200' hill climb, from miles 6.5 to 10.5. At mile 8 we entered the Sulham Woods, a UK Area of Outstanding National Beauty with a host of stately trees. My pace slowed as I climbed the hill on uneven surfaces. We pop out of the woods and run through farm fields. I am happily running uphill through the fields! Then on to Little Heath Road, a nice stretch of asphalt before Twizzler Woods at mile 11 and the aid station at mile 12.

Suddenly we are back on a towpath, -it's the Kennet and Avon Canal! The sun is out and so are the canal boats. The

canals were used to transport goods during the 19th and 20th centuries. The traditional wooden narrowboats were working boats, the lifeline of the transport system in the UK. Once railroad haulage became more cost-effective the canals started to fall into disrepair. The system found a new life and is heavily used by restored canal boats. It's slow traveling, I passed this one in no time!

The next highlight is Madejski Stadium, the home of the Reading Football Club, a team in the Championship League. We ran the roads and I picked up my first nutrition package at aid station #3, perfect timing at 18 miles. Then the course returned to scenic fields and back lanes. I looked forward to aid station #4 and my restock of gels, I needed the energy boost. I was still moving but my left leg was lacking in power. I hit 26.7 miles with a time of 4:55, much slower than normal but I would finish!!

Those last five miles took another hour to complete, I did my share of walking to get to the finish minimizing injury to my unhappy hamstring. It was woodland running until we hit the last stretch of road to return to the village of Sonning and the Berkshire Sports Club...still very scenic!

I was so happy to see Bob at the finish line! I could have been much faster if I had been in better health. I had doubts due to my injury but slow and steady got me to my goal! Georgia and Cheryl, two very happy gals!

Chapter 37: 2020 Plym Trail Marathon

Date: September 12, 2020, 9:30 am, Clearbrook, UK

Weather: Overcast, 33F at start, high of 58F

Participation: 24 marathon, 30 half marathon

2 for 1: The 124th Boston Marathon Virtual & the 2020 Plym Trail Marathon

Two for one? Virtual marathon? Is this running anarchy?

The Boston Marathon was initially rescheduled from April 20, 2020, to September 14, 2020, due to the Covid-19 pandemic. On May 28th, the Mayor of Boston announced that the 124th running of the Boston Marathon would no longer be held on September 14th. They felt that they could not safely run the race during the Covid-19 pandemic. Instead, the race would be a virtual event with participants running between September 7 -14th. What is a virtual event? You register for the race, run the 26.2 miles any place you like, submit proof, and the race organizers send you a medal. I am not a big fan of the concept since a virtual event does not count as a "race" but I felt like I had to run it since I was an active member of the Hyland's Boston Marathon Legacy running team. It would be my fifth consecutive Boston Marathon; my fourth consecutive Boston with Hyland's, I didn't want to miss it! I decided to look for a real race and run the virtual event at the same time…. "two for one".

Several of us were interested in doing the Boston Virtual event so in mid-June, we signed up for Revel Cottonwood, a downhill race in Utah that had been postponed to September 12. Utah had very few Covid-19 cases and was allowing events to take place. By mid-July, Revel announced the cancellation of the Cottonwood event due to Covid-19. Bob and I also got word that our August flight back to the US was canceled. On the bright side, this opened up the possibility of an extended stay in the UK.

As luck would have it, the perfect local race appeared on my radar! Davey Greene, the Chair of the 100 Marathon Club in the UK, was hosting a race weekend on the Plym Trail just north of Plymouth, UK on September 12th and 13th. I am a provisional member of the club and due to join when I reach my 100th marathon, so it seemed like the perfect opportunity to meet some club members. I had never been on the Plym Trail but it was in Dartmoor National Park and was bound to be scenic. The race strictly limited the number of participants, so it seemed like it had a good chance of going ahead. I had my "two for one" race!

Things started to get exciting a week before race day when the Boston 2020 Team Hyland's Playbook was released. Hyland's is an official sponsor of the Boston Marathon and for the past four years, they have assembled a team of runners to share in the Boston Marathon experience. I have been a Legacy member each year; in 2017, they assembled a team of women runners to celebrate the 50th anniversary of women running the Boston Marathon, in 2018 the team theme was teachers and I was able to share the experience with my friend Natalie, a teacher from West Virginia, 2019 was the year of healers and 2020 is the year for builders of change.

The playbook allowed us to stay involved in Hyland's Boston experience. We were encouraged to send photos of our race. Hyland's developed augmented reality tools to personalize our experience with things like start and finish line banners which you add to your photos. They put together posters for us to see our teammates together. Race day was made special with the opportunity to submit bragging rights or quirky achievements from race day. Hyland's kept the virtual race fun for the team!

The Boston Marathon also had a virtual app we could use to keep track of our mileage. I stuck with my reliable Garmin watch. The app did an amazing job of trying to replicate as much of the Boston race week experience as they could. The expo was virtual. They had online content all week long, they sent a daily newsletter to keep participants motivated. We could download our bib, the Boston course mile markers plus a start line and finish line tape. It also had an audio component which I did not try, but you could get audio cues during your race, including the Wellesley Scream Tunnel. It would have been amazing to use these features, but my race was in an area with no cell phone reception. It is the price you pay for being up on remote Dartmoor National Park!

Bob and I arrived early on race day so we could check out the trail. The race started at Clearbrook, a very small village on the northern edge of Dartmoor National Park, an Area of Outstanding Natural Beauty. Dartmoor is one of the last great wilderness areas left in the UK. It is an area of open moorland and craggy stone formations that is known for the

wild ponies roaming the countryside. There were a few up the road from the start line!

The Plym Trail is a rail-trail that follows the old Great Western Railway line through a heavily wooded valley. The rail line opened in 1859 and closed to passengers in 1962. The railroad traversed some difficult terrain so I will be passing over three large viaduct bridges and one tunnel, all designed by England's most famous engineer, IK Brunel.

Photos of the viaduct bridges sold me on the scenery! I will go up and down the trail twice so will pass each bridge four times!

This happens to be the 400th year since the sailing of the Mayflower. This weekend there was an unveiling of a full-sized automated, unmanned trimaran that will recreate the crossing from Plymouth to America. It is part of a larger celebration in Plymouth of the Mayflower and its voyage. If I can't be in Boston, then Plymouth's Plym Trail is a great symbolic substitute!

The race started at the village hall in Clearbrook. The marathon starts at 9:30, the half at 10:30. The marathon has about 25 runners; it's the smallest event I have ever done! It has a friendly feel, and the race director assigned me bib #99 in honor of my "almost there-100 marathons" status. I received my bib after a temperature check at the registration table, a new first for me. The waiting area, toilets, and hot drinks were available inside the village hall, so pleasant!

We had an outdoor race briefing where I learned another runner was doing the Boston virtual also! We divide up into groups of five runners and then left six feet between groups as we moved to the start.

There was a short out and back run out of the village before we got on to the Plym Trail. There was just one human gate (a gate that allows bikers and walkers to pass into an area that is fenced) on the entire trail, and the race marshal held it open on the first pass, so nice!

Three miles into the course we enter one of the Brunel projects I was looking forward to, the Shaugh Tunnel. It extends about a half-mile through the rock and seems a tight fit for a train engine. I laughed when I learned the tunnel was only recently

fitted out with interior lights! Just beyond the tunnel is the Shaugh bridge. By mile 4, we are passing over the lovely Bickleigh and Riverford viaduct bridges, sweet!

At mile 6 we have entered the Plymbridge Woods, managed by The National Trust. It is the most scenic part of the trail. We cross the Cann Viaduct bridge, spanning the Cann Quarry. Miners worked the slate quarry since 1683, but now it is the quiet home of a pair of Peregrine falcons! Falcons have been nesting on the cliffs since the 1960s. On the bridge I pass informational signage and a binocular scope to watch the birds; It's all part of the Plym Peregrine project.

Next, we go over the Plym Bridge, a grade II listed bridge made of granite with a history back to 1238! The bridge was used to get access to the local granite and slate quarries. There is much more activity at this end of the trail, families out biking, walkers, and of course, I am seeing the speedsters returning from the upcoming Coypool aid station!

It has been six miles of downhill running by the time I arrive at the turnaround at Coypool. I tried to keep my pace in check so I would have something in the tank for the end of the race. The run back uphill was better than I expected, no walking and I cross the halfway point in 2:09.

I was warned that the second lap would be tough and it was. I struggled to head uphill the last six miles. I overtook a few runners so the hills around Polperro have been a benefit to my training. Pre-race, I was hoping I could achieve a 4:10-4:15 finish since the race was rumored to be flat with an asphalt surface and the field of runners was small. I adjusted my estimate as soon as Bob and I walked the first half-mile of the trail. In the end, it was an elevation gain of 1,083 feet and a finish time of 4:29:45!

~on the upside I came in as the second female and was cheered by a herd of sheep. I received the most appropriate medal this running beekeeper has in her medal collection! I hope to be back in December 2020 for the Merry Xmas Marathon...

Chapter 38: Not Quite London Marathon

Date: October 4, 2020, 8:35 am start, Staines, UK

Weather: Rain and cloudy, 48F at start, high of 58F

Participation: 60 marathoners

2 for 1: The 40th Race, Virtual London Marathon & The Nearly But Not Quite London Marathon

She stood in the 'Virtual' storm and when the wind did not blow her away, she adjusted her sails!!   ~*from Wendy*

My **100th Marathon**, my ultimate goal, I needed a plan, a revised Covid-19 plan... In 2019, I selected a race on the Cornish Coastal Path for August 2020, but Covid-19 dashed that and the race canceled in late May. Life settled a bit over the summer, but there was still a two-week quarantine for international travelers coming to the UK so no hope that my US running friends could join me. The UK government currently limits social gatherings to six people indoors and outdoors, so I would have a small celebration at best. On August 7, 2020, the London Marathon announced that the 40th race would be for elite runners only, the mass participation event would be a virtual race held on October 4. In New York, the state was requiring a two-week quarantine for travelers returning from 38 other states, and no races were being run locally. My **100th Marathon** plan seemed obvious, I would find a marathon on October 4th in the UK and have my family with me at the finish.

On August 7th, in a panic, I signed up for a race in Reading called the Magic Runabout. It was a seven-hour race, with participants running as many laps as they can. It wasn't ideal since it was the same stretch of the Thames River I ran in July and it wasn't a marathon, but at least I found a long-distance race for October 4th near London.

In early September I found an alternative, a marathon at Eton College with a flat and fast run around Dorney Lake. It was the first marathon to be held at this location but it looked perfect so I signed up. I contacted the race director and let him know it would be my 100th!

It was also time to sign up for the Virtual London Marathon, another "2 for 1." A contingent of the Looe Pioneers was signed up, so October 4th was going to be a big day!

In late September, the race information packet came for Dorney Lake. Due to Covid-19 spectators will no longer be allowed! UGHH!!!!! I won't run my 100th without my family there! Now what? This is so stressful!

I looked to find yet another race and got lucky! Saturn Running decided to offer two races on October 4th, so I switched from the Magic Runabout to the Nearly But Not Quite London Marathon, which would be held on the Thames Path at Staines-upon-Thames. It was a three-loop course with a start and finish at the Thames Side Brewery, ~perfect! Jessica has a very good friend that is also a runner, Nacho, he joined the race too, even better!

As race day came, I started feeling a tremendous sense of emptiness; I felt sad that my US friends could not join my **100th Marathon** race. There was no official race in Cornwall, so no option to run with the Looe Pioneer virtual London Marathoners. Imagine my disappointment! I got the notion in my head to have family and friends send a race cheer or words of support to Bob, which he would put in an envelope and hand to me at my race. I would open it there. My race would lack pomp and circumstance, but it would be rich with emotion and personal connection! I ordered balloons, bunting, horns, and started planning my cake. Our bubble was going to do a **100th Marathon** celebration in style!

It started raining two days before the race, and it just kept on raining…. race day, more rain, and a change in the racecourse. Can you believe this?! Instead of three laps of 8.75 miles with a lovely tour through Runnymede (remember the Magna Carta!) we would do six loops running north of Staines on the Thames Path and avoid the mud and water-logged sections of the trail.

We nervously arrived at the race start and found the setup to be great! There was a covered garage right next to the brewery and the race director had set up the start line right next to it. The family would stay warm, dry, and close to the car. Josie's mate, Zach, had arrived with runner dad, Nacho, and Rohan. The day was going to be fun for everyone!!

I was scheduled for an 8:30 am start, so I put on my virtual London Marathon bib, picked up my official bib #100, and was ready to go. I had to track my virtual run using the London Marathon app, so carried my phone in the rain, a true test for Ziplock bags! Bob handed me my first

packet of race cheers, I was pumped up and ready to go! The race director was releasing groups of six runners at a time to start the race. My 8:30 group was full so we got a special 8:35 start, just me, Nacho, and another runner! ~Sweet!!!

I fumbled around a bit the first mile trying to get comfortable in the rain, carrying water, food, phone, envelope, face mask, and my electrolyte kit. After mile 1, I decided that each mile I would pull out a cheer card from my envelope and think about that person for the mile. Bob's first card for me was from my niece and nephew, Carolyn and John, a perfect choice as they have inspired me from the beginning of my running career:

IF YOU ARE TIRED…. **GO FASTER AND SMILE!!!**

IF YOU ARE FEELING GOOD…. **GO EVEN FASTER AND SMILE MORE!!**

YOU
ARE: **STRONG FLUID PREPARED EFFICIENT FOCUSED FAST HAPPY BRAVE PROUD RESILIENT DISCIPLINED INSPIRING**

THIS IS NUMBER **100!!**

YOU ARE A PART OF A **SMALL, ELITE MINORITY!**

FINISH STRONG

WE ARE BEYOND **PROUD OF YOU!**

It did the trick; I was smiling and the cold rain no longer bothered me. I felt a glow inside and I could hear Carolyn and John in my head. I didn't run faster, instead, I ran to enjoy the time I

had with them during our personal mile. I continued to open the cheer cards from the family for the next miles and ended with a final note from my nephew, Roy, *"Congratulations on running your 100th marathon! What an accomplishment of pure physical and mental strength. That is about 2,620 miles of marathon racing. To put that in perspective, that is more miles than a flight from New York City to Los Angeles, CA!"*

What fun my first loop had been!

The next several groups of cheer cards were from friends; each one struck a chord with me. Some made me laugh, some made me tear up, some made me reminisce and they all made me feel cherished! I couldn't have felt more motivated to cross a finish line than I did that day! It made for a very emotional run, I had to dig deep to stay focused on the physical running of the race.   ~No falls, please!

Every time we finished a loop I would run past my family and 50 meters down I would hit the turn around and run past them again. We got the hang of it, I would yell out what I need and Bob would hand me a package, Josie and Zach would high-five and cheer for me while Jess took

photos. There may not have been many spectators on the course, but I only had eyes for my cheer squad!

I hit the halfway mark at 2:10 and was glowing. Nacho had lapped me already and watching him run was a thing of beauty! The Thames River Path was flat with a mix of terrain, mostly asphalt with some cinder sections. Typically, we would share the path with the public, but with the rain, we had the trail almost to ourselves. Out on the river, we saw a few rowers but not much activity.

As I came in finishing my fourth loop, I was feeling the run. I was stiff and my hamstring was giving me problems again. Bob yelled, "it's the last lap, right?" and my only response was... "I wish!" I could not imagine running another two laps! Nacho had a great run and finished first place in three hours. I would be lucky to get in at 4:30 so they would have a long wait!

I picked up some gels and tried to find a new attitude as I opened my next set of cheer cards. Wendy's said, ***"She stood in the 'Virtual' storm and*** *when the wind did not blow her away, she adjusted her sails!"* I took this to heart and got a second wind for the fifth lap. The rain stopped, I shed my coat and adjusted my sails. It would not be fast, but I set sail.

I was in complete control until 24.91 miles and then it happened, the great hamstring revolt. My entire left leg was locked up in one big spasm. The pain pierced through my hamstring and then shot right down to my ankles. I stooped over on the side of the course in tears. I tried stretching it out; I tried walking, but nothing gave me relief.

Several minutes later, I walked slowly, so slowly that the walkers were zooming by me expressing sympathy. As the pain settled down, I tried a light jog, but that was too much and the cramp came back with its full force. I had one more mile to go and I couldn't imagine getting to the finish line.

This is not the way I want to cross the finish line, stop cramping now!!!!!

> *It doesn't matter where you're going;*
>
> *It doesn't matter how far you go;*
>
> *It doesn't matter the pace you travel;*
>
> *As long as you run the run.*
>
> ~*from Gerald*

I took my nephew, Jerry's words to heart and proudly picked up the pace to a very slow jog, I kept going. Eventually, I neared Josie and Zach at the finish line, only to find out I still had to make it 50 meters to the turnaround and come back again. The push past the finish line did not go well, and I was cramping again at the turnaround. As the pain returned, I couldn't hold back the tears! I saw that Josie and Bob had set up a finish banner for me, so I walked as fast as I could...

The agony is all over my face in the next photo. Josie summarized it best, **"Get my Grandma a wheelchair!"**

Cramps eventually go away, and soon Josie and I were happily collecting my finisher medal. Jessica had coordinated with Thames Side Brewery next door so we could have our post-race celebration with them. We all settled in for celebratory drinks. The talk turned to the merrier moments of the race... Nacho as 1st Place runner and me as a **100th Marathon**

finisher. It didn't take long before I was scheming with Nacho for another race weekend, post-Covid-19, after my hamstring tendinosis heals, ~maybe Vilnius in Lithuania or Skopje in Macedonia or Rome???? We'll find a race with a marathon plus a 10K for Bob & Jim and a kids run. ~How quickly marathoners forget the pain of our labor!

My mother was a professional cake decorator so cakes are important to us. My **100th Marathon** celebration cake was no exception! Jess made my favorite white cake with chocolate icing! Josie came up with the decorating ideas, bunting with the words "Well Done Grandma" and the honey bees on flowers. I made the blue Saucony running shoes symbolic of my race day shoes.

It was an emotional day filled with extreme highs and lows, but nothing matched the pure joy of sharing a piece of this cake and a beer with my running bubble.

~Many thanks to Bob, Jess, Josie, Zack, Nacho, and Rohan!!

Afterword

I grew up when opportunities for women were opening up, so I took advantage. My mother raised me in the '70s, I believed in the Equal Rights Amendment guaranteeing equal rights to women and assumed it was law. I matured when girls were exploring the world of sports. Young women could pursue a career of their choice. I was fortunate enough to be surrounded by women that pushed beyond society's limits. I didn't realize we were supposed to have boundaries, so I just crossed them.

I had the chance to play local club softball because my mother started a girl's league, she made that opportunity available for me where none existed. The club shaped so many young girls! I attended high school after Title IX passed, funding for women's sport was finally made available. Title IX says that "No person in the United States shall, on the basis of sex, be excluded from participation in, be denied the benefits of, or be subjected to discrimination under any education program or activity receiving Federal financial assistance." This funding gave me the option to participate in a girl's high school sports program. Girls could be active in sports and blend it into a healthy lifestyle. We were breaking barriers.

After High School, I chose to pursue architecture. I was one of a handful of women in the program. A single mother like me entering the university program was unheard of! I graduated and entered the field in 1984 at a time when less than 4% of architects were women. The ratio of women to men in architecture school is almost 50/50 now! Society is changing as women participate in new ways.

I felt the need to re-invent myself after retiring from architecture in 2008. The reinvention started with a 1,000-mile four-month-long sea kayak trip around Vancouver Island with my husband. Day in and day out, our minds relaxed and our bodies grew physically stronger. Our nomadic lifestyle meant a daily search for drinking water and campsites. We learned to take nature in stride as we embraced the rhythm of waves and tides. We were finding a different way to exist.

Eventually, it was running that took the center stage of my post-retirement life. With a pair of running shoes you can run, it's much easier than loading up the car with all the kayak gear! I took my first jog in 2010, did my first marathon in November of 2012, and now I identify myself as a long-distance runner through and through. 100 marathons, with 80 road races and 20 trail races, 90 marathons, and 10 ultras…I like the proportions, I love entire the story!

In each race report I am reminded of my growth as a runner as I advanced through several stages of my running career, The Newbie, The Maniac, The Speedster, The Ultra Marathoner. I remember the mistakes, the lessons, and the discoveries I made over the years. The big question remains, where to go from here?

Glossary of Terms

Bonking: verb, hitting the wall or bonking is the point at which the body's glycogen stores are depleted and the body starts to fatigue and burn fat, making each step towards the finish line a vicious battle of mind over body. It's an uncomfortable sensation – legs feel heavy, body drained, and the mind spent.

BQ: noun, an acronym for Boston Qualifier, used to describe a marathon time that qualifies a person for entry into the Boston Marathon.

Charley horse: noun, charley horse is the common name for a muscle spasm or cramp. Muscle spasms can occur in any muscle in the body but often happen in the leg. When a muscle is in spasm, it contracts without your control and does not relax.

Chip time: noun, A technology for sensing and recording the finishing times of all the runners in a race. It's much more accurate and can easily deal with the old problem of many runners finishing nearly at once in a big, crowded race. The "chip" is a tiny electronic chip that's programmed with your specific runner identification.

Corrals: noun, Corrals are used to sort runners into appropriate pace groups, especially at large races. They help to manage the flow of runners and guarantee that everyone moves forward at the same speed.

Faceplant: noun, an instance of falling face-first into or onto something.

Garmin: noun, Garmin is a manufacturer of sports watches. I used the Garmin Forerunner and then after Crater Lake Marathon the Fenix series. The watches are designed to accurately measure distance, speed, heart rate (optional), time, altitude, and pace, all of which can be important to athletes in training.

GI: noun, an acronym for gastrointestinal, the most frequent exercise-induced gastrointestinal symptoms are short-lived abdominal pain, heartburn and acid reflux, vomiting, diarrhea, and bloody diarrhea.

GU: noun, Gu running gel, GU Energy Labs produces performance sports nutrition products, most notably energy gels. Usually consumed during endurance events, the gels are designed to be quickly and easily digested.

Marathon: noun, 26.2 miles; According to legend, in 490 B.C., a Greek soldier name Pheidippides ran the distance from the site of the battle of Marathon to Athens, where he died after the Greek victory over the Persians.

Pace band: noun, A pace band is a wristband, sometimes made of a strip of waterproof paper, that lists expected split times for a running race. When used in conjunction with a stopwatch, a pace band can assist athletes in maintaining a steady pace throughout the race.

Pacer: noun, A pacer when running is useful in more ways than one. Generally, a pacer is an experienced runner that runs at a set speed in a race, typically a long-distance event. This helps you finish at your desired time.

PR: noun, an acronym for a personal record, referring to a person's best time in a race of a specific distance.

VO2 Max: noun, the maximum rate of oxygen consumption measured during incremental exercise; that is, the exercise of increasing intensity. The name is derived from three abbreviations: "V" for volume, "O2" for oxygen, and "max" for maximum.

Acknowledgments

I have been supported in my running by many people along the way. I have made lifelong friends in my local running communities. Those that have gotten me through difficult races have left a deep, positive impact. I named a few of them in my race reports but not every race is reported so not every moment is captured. I want to thank each of you for the enrichment our adventures have added to my life. In your way, you have helped me to write and publish this book.

I would especially like to thank the recipients of my race report emails. I received so much genuine positive feedback from each of you. It was very much appreciated and encouraged me to keep writing. "I felt like I was there with you!" and "You should write a book!" were favorites.

I have had the unconditional support of my husband, Bob on this runabout. I couldn't have asked for a more giving husband. So much so that he also took up running after our Hawaii adventure. He has lived through most of the races, read through every race report, and was my sounding board for this book. He also became my photographer, picking me out of the masses and capturing that special moment as I run by! I would not have finished this book without his devotion to the final product!

My daughter, Jessica had the patience through the years to travel along to many of my European races. With that comes the endless runner-centric focus such as; what food to eat, how will I sneak in my morning run, I must get sleep, how to get to the race start, where will they be spectating? She has always been there to support me and imparts her respect for my accomplishments to our granddaughter. That is life's greatest gift.

My niece, Carolyn, and her husband John were my first advisors. I saw a marathon training plan posted on their fridge. I had no idea what it took to properly train and was so intrigued! Little did John know he had opened Pandora's Box and that one day I would become a US Track and Field running coach and develop training plans. Carolyn lent me my first running book, *Marathon Woman* by Katherine Switzer. It was the perfect book to start my exploration of marathoning. She also gave me my first running journal which started a lifelong habit of keeping track of my training statistics. Every kernel of advice has been absorbed. I credit them with getting me to the start line of my first marathon; then on to LA, Edinburgh, and Chicago for the elusive Boston qualifying time.

My massage therapist, Julia, has been like a life coach pushing my limits, keeping my body healthy, and offering her friendship. I will never forget my first visit to her home and the wall of medals she had hanging in her massage room. I couldn't believe that one person could run that much and stay so healthy. In 2014 at the Shamrock Marathon in Virginia Beach, I watched her receive her plaque from the 50 States Marathon club for completing marathons in all 50 states. The Shamrock Marathon would be my 8th marathon, most people in the room had completed ten times that. I would get there one day!

I thank Christine whose cheer card at my 100th marathon was "now finish the book!" Your consistent encouragement kept me focused, I can't thank you enough. Through the years you read my race reports and always wanted more, you believed that a book was in me.

Sharon, reporter and my weekly running mate, our vigorous discussions, your comments on my introduction and chapter lead-ins helped to hone my writing style. The honest opinions on what you enjoy reading had an impact on my tactical approach.

I thank Phil and Lorna for the advice on publishing and sales. I had much to learn and your lessons saved me from more than a few setbacks. Lorna, author and non-runner, your pre-publication read through and feedback was invaluable and encouraging. Your investment in my success showed the mark of a true mentor!

Sue, artist, and teacher, your read through and advice on graphics added clarity to the race reports. Your critique and encouragement on the text helped pave the way to the completion of the final draft. Thank you for lending me your keen eye.

A large part of the motivation for this book came from Bill, you laid the foundation. You encouraged me to archive my early race reports and package them as a legacy for my family. You also offered to assist me in publishing my work, your patience is boundless. Your advice on the production and printing of a book was invaluable. Your desire to see a complete book kept me motivated for the last five years.

This was a group project; I thank everyone that contributed to its success.

Printed in Great Britain
by Amazon